T0209353

THE ASCENDING MORAL COMPASS

THE KEY TO
SPIRITUAL FAITH AND TRUTH

MAKI JAHANA

WESTBOW
P R E S S®
A DIVISION OF THOMAS NELSON
& ZONDERVAN

WestBow Press books may be ordered through booksellers or by contacting:

WestBow Press
A Division of Thomas Nelson & Zondervan
1663 Liberty Drive
Bloomington, IN 47403
www.westbowpress.com
844-714-3454

Scripture quotations are taken from the Holy Bible, King James Version (Public Domain).

ISBN: 979-8-3850-0669-4 (sc)
ISBN: 979-8-3850-0670-0 (hc)
ISBN: 979-8-3850-0668-7 (e)

Library of Congress Control Number: 2023916850

Print information available on the last page.

WestBow Press rev. date: 10/24/2023

CONTENTS

ACKNOWLEDGMENTS

I am grateful and humbled to be able to write this book. I am not worthy to even call his name, but his compassion and mercy toward humanity saved me. With the Holy Spirit in my life, I learned how to examine my mind, thoughts, and feelings to avoid emotional setbacks.

My inheritance is inside me. The Holy Spirit teaches and guides me and the faithful ones who live totally in divine connection with God and the innermost being linked with all people, godly beings, and all forms of life.

I am grateful for my children's support during this time. I would like to thank them—Nika, Kirk, Jamal, and Shamar—and my grandchildren, especially my eldest granddaughter, A 'Shylah, and her little sister and baby brother. They are the reasons I dedicate my life to learning about the Highest. I desire to leave a legacy of inspiration for them to know God and give reverence to our Creator of the heavens and the earth.

I would have never come into the knowledge of my Savior were it not for his faithful servants. They have changed my life in so many ways, and I thank them for sharing the Word. They have taught me to accept what I cannot change and forgive others. It will release me from stress and free me from fear.

Thanks to Iwata, Akea Beka, and Elder Ricketts for inspiring me to keep the law and the Sabbath day holy to inspire faith in others and to search the scripture for myself.

I also thank my friends and the library staff for their support. There are too many to name.

1

ADJUSTING MY MORAL COMPASS: THE KEY TO SPIRITUAL FAITH AND TRUTH

Our journey starts in the matrix of our mothers' wombs. It was written long before I even knew that I had a mighty Creator who loved me and was the director of my life.

I was not living according to what was expected of me. I was a lost sheep in the wilderness. Not only that, but I also embraced the seductions of this fallen world and tried to survive on my own. My moral compass was turned upside down, broken, and unable to be used until I learned to be obedient to the owner of my compass.

I did not understand the opportunity I was given. I found it difficult to leave my dad, my friends, and my community. I was extremely attached to my dad, and it hurt to leave him because I loved him so much. This caused me to rebel against the sudden migration from the island to a foreign country when I was twelve years old. I set my mind against the new country that had welcomed me.

Furthermore, I was living according to what I saw around me. I had my first child at age nineteen and then got married when I had my second child. We were both immature and had no clue how to nurture children. He and I were too young to even understand the responsibility of raising children. Considered an illegal, his path in life was not easy for him as a young man. Quite often, it led him into trouble. Regardless of the difficulties, we got married to keep the family together. But due to unseen circumstances, he was deemed unfit for society and went back to the island, even though we pleaded for his presence in the children's lives.

After years of hardship and many struggles in the province, I moved to a big city in another province, hoping for a better life. A family member provided a place for us to stay until we could get our own place. But moving to a big city did not go as well as I expected. I got a divorce after about three years because there was no hope of reuniting. I had no work during the first year in the big city and no income. I was not qualified to receive assistant or even to go to college because one must live in the province for at least a year to qualify for college or any kind of government assistance. I worked at various factory jobs and sold drugs on the side. I used what other skills I had to generate extra income doing ladies' hair at their homes. And I got to know the city and met a lot of people.

I waited for one year and got into college. We received some financial support, and my children got subsidized day care. The money was not enough to keep up with day-care fees, food, clothes, and other things necessary to maintain them. It took a great toll on me just to find the bus fare to go to classes. I continued to sell drugs.

I was driven to do whatever it took to improve my life. I got an offer to make real money, big money, fast money. The deal was so good that I took it. It was a vacation with pay for a weekend. I returned from "vacation" two years later. I completely messed up my life and had to start again.

When I returned home, I promised to do better and stay out of trouble. I got a job working for a travel agency. Months passed, and my children and my family forgave me for leaving them so long.

I felt lonely and started dating again. I met a wonderful man and soon got pregnant. That relationship failed. By the age of thirty-eight, I was a single parent of four—one girl and three boys—and a grandmother. After so many setbacks, I chose to stop dating and focus on my children and work. I became a workaholic. My primary job was as a medical tech. The two part-time jobs in different hospitals were my primary sources of income. At night, I would clean a medical building and had a casual job every other weekend cleaning an endoscopic scope in the north.

I usually worked nights, days, and weekends until my youngest son, who was five years old at the time, waited up for me all night because he refused to go to sleep until he saw me at least once. It touched my heart to see that he cared. So I made some changes to my busy work schedule for them.

I sought help from friends and family, but no one was available to help. One friend suggested that I hire his mother, who lived in a different country. I spoke to her, and she was willing to come and assist me. I immediately sent her a ticket. She was a major help to us. She was like a mother to my children and a great helper and friend to me. Now the children were with an adult while I went to work. I did not worry so much anymore.

There was no need for my old character anymore, and I felt fully confident that I could make a brighter future for my family. Our helper was an older lady with grown children. One of her sons came to visit, and we welcomed him into our home. He was not working at the time. I offered to pay him if he would help me with cleaning the medical offices. I paid him for whatever work he did.

Things were going very well. I decided to save toward buying a house for my children and me. I took all the shifts I could get at work and never took vacations or holidays. I did not think of doing anything but work, and I bought a house. In 2006, we moved into our new house. It was a four-bedroom detached house with a complete basement in a quiet neighborhood. It had a huge backyard for the children to play in and a full fence. We had a beautiful home with enough space for two cars to park. The children had their own rooms. I worked for eight years to maintain it, and then I took a break.

During this time, I grew to have feelings for my helper's son. He displayed a great character: warm, kind, and faithful. He was willing, immensely helpful, and patient. My youngest sons loved him very much, and I thought he was the perfect fit to be a stepfather to my children. I decided to go on dates with him.

He was shy at first and did not talk a lot. I thought he was trying not to say the wrong thing, or he was unsure how to deal with the children. It was new for him because he had no children of his own. He knew what was missing, and he would find ways to fill that gap. I was willing, open, and ready to share my life with him; he seemed faithful, loving, and genuine. I was willing to work with him, and we got married in 2013.

A few months later, I was in a car accident that changed my life. And it saved my life.

The car accident was in 2014. I was out of work and confined to my bed, physically and mentally disabled. My choice of work was limited. At the time, I was on disability payments, which was my only income to pay all my bills. After two years, I was unemployed and very depressed. I started to look for business ideas to help me because I had to pay the mortgage, and it was time for renewal. I had not worked since the accident. I had no savings or credit, and no bank would consider me fit for a renewal or a loan.

I affiliated myself with many business opportunities as I tried to get back on my feet to make money to pay my bills and mortgage. My disability check was not enough. I was falling into a worsening depression. I became withdrawn and felt hopeless. During this time, I kept getting sicker and sicker. Either my legs were swollen or my head and back kept hurting. I could not sit, stand, or walk too long. My body hurt so much. It still depresses me when I think about the situation I was facing. I was seen by several doctors and therapists for months, but nothing changed. I decided I needed to stop everything and take a break from all my life responsibilities. It was hard for me to sleep every night when I saw how my life had changed since the accident. The children and the family home had changed too. I had a child support court case, my divorce case was pending, and a child suddenly got sick. It was like taking bitter pills that left me restless and broken. But I had to deal with it. And the thoughts of becoming homeless were too overwhelming for me to explain.

One day I decided to shed my pride and talk to my family doctor. He gave me more pills and referred me to a physiatrist to talk to them about what I was dealing with. I decided to face my fears and took his advice. I signed up for a twelve-week session with the physiatrist. It was ridiculously hard at first because, in my culture, this was only for mentally challenged people. Even though they had recommended that I see a physiatrist after my accident. I did not feel right. But I was stuck in a situation with nowhere to turn, and my moral compass was being challenged.

During my six sessions of therapy, I came to realize that I just needed a break from everything around me; I had never taken a personal break before. My children were of age now and had proved themselves to be responsible enough to be left alone for a few weeks.

For a few days, I slept on whether to sell the family home or find a job. It was coming down to crunch time. I tried to think of a family member or friend I could trust to take over the mortgage. But I found no one trustworthy or qualified to help. This was my first and only home, and I did not know what to do or where to start. I had a meeting with my children, and we talked about selling, refinancing, or going back to renting. We agreed to refinance the house for the first time. It seemed like a great idea. Plus, the upgrade of the home would add to its value if I later decided to sell it.

Not knowing the procedure necessary to qualify for refinancing was another dilemma for me because only my name was on the mortgage. Remember: I had no work since 2014, no savings, and imperfect credit. I set my mind to venturing into different business meetings and events, trying to understand how to get some support or help in making the best financial decision for our family home. I met so many people who were experienced and knowledgeable in helping people who had challenges with their credit. I spoke to a few people and chose one who seemed qualified for this dilemma. He agreed to try his best to help me refinance the home. Plus, he suggested he could help me fix my credit.

Pay Attention to the Fine Print on a Compass

I found out I had enough equity in the home from the refinancing to upgrade and pay the mortgage for one year. I took the deal because I was down and out, but this new opportunity would help me to pay my mortgage and bills. I was $100,000 away from paying off my home, but … Then, without fully understanding what was ahead, I jumped into this massive project. I was so excited to know that I was qualified and could pay my mortgage and bills. It felt good.

I was pleased with myself as a single parent of four and a beautiful granddaughter. Likewise, I had big plans to refurbish our family home after twelve years. I had not done anything major on the house since I bought it in 2006. I decided to do a renovation of the entire house. I hired a real estate agent; he was the same person who got me approved. He advised me on the best way to approach the renovation. I borrowed enough money from the equity in the house to put toward the mortgage, pay bills, and travel in the future. We met the agent a few times before deciding to go ahead with the work. He hired a team of people and started the work on the home in March 2017.

During the first stage, I was calm and cool. But then it became so overwhelming and disappointing when two workers had a verbal disagreement in my basement that almost turned into a fistfight on the first day of work at my home. I felt unsure about the workers' ability to get the work done on time. I felt they did not want to take orders from me, maybe because I was a woman.

But since this was our home, I needed to make sure the plans were what we all agreed on, and they should stick to the contract to get the place ready on time as planned. I did not realize it would take so much mental and physical energy to organize the children and all the things in the house. Day and night I talked to the agent, the contractors, and the children to get things in order. We had no place to stay during the renovation; we had to live through it. We needed a storage place for all the things in the house except our beds. I felt like the principal at a school for disobedient children. It was more than I bargained for. I had to give everyone a task and then encourage them to keep focused. Every so often, I checked to make sure the tasks were done. The children were more receptive than I thought they would be. We worked as a team to get the home ready for the contractors and stayed out of their way.

We were happy about the renovation of the house, even though the contractors were dragging their feet. It took two months before I saw what I requested, with lots of stops in between. However, I allowed them to do what was best for all. I had frequent mental outbursts and breakdowns. It was too much for me. Finally, I was getting annoyed with everything and started to feel sick and nervous. I was trapped with my wants and did not remember what I really needed. I made some plans to travel to my homeland for a while. I ran for cover.

2

THE GREAT CATCH

Things turn out best for the people who make
the best out-of-the-way things turn out.

—Art Linkletter

I finally decided to take a break. I asked my eldest son to go with me on the trip because he needed a break too. I booked a two-week, all-inclusive air and hotel at the Royal Caribbean vacation resort on the island. It was a trip well deserved, and we took advantage of the opportunity to leave my only daughter and the rest of the children at home to oversee the contractors.

It was a dream of mine, and I was happy to share it with my eldest son. This was his first vacation. It was our first time going on a two-week, all-inclusive vacation anywhere. But it was not our first time on the Island. The resort was breathtaking and luxurious. I was in a new place and feeling like a queen, ready to sit around and do nothing. There was a lot of food, drinks, and desserts of all kinds and entertainment day and night. I could feel the fun in the atmosphere, people always coming and going. Their grounds were well-kept, and I admired their flower garden. There were pools in every corner of the resort, and the ocean area was reserved for their guests only. I liked the different cabins all over the grounds that were used by their guests. And room service was available at the tip of my fingers. That is what I enjoyed the most.

A few days later, my son and I took a boat ride with one of the workers out into the deep ocean. I was scared at first to go but still fascinated to see and experience such a magnificent boat ride. On the following days, we went to the different sides of the beach. One day, we planned to go swimming, and my son walked out into the ocean. I thought he was going for a swim, but he kept walking. He went so far out in the water that a man in his canoe stopped him. As they were talking, I took some pictures and videotaped the moment because I could not believe the water was that shallow, or he was that tall. It was amazing to see.

The resort had many activities, including tennis courts, basketball courts, and exercise classes in the pools or on the sand. You could participate in yoga, Pilates, and games. There was even the chance to go onstage to sing or dance with the team of the resort. I was not interested in anything but relaxing on the beach with my book and my headset, listening to my kind of music.

An Absolute Vegan Went on an All-Inclusive, All-You-Can-Eat Vacation

There were many choices in the foods offered at the open buffet. They did not have a vegan buffet, but all the salads, vegetables, bread, and fruit you could think of were available. While I am not a big drinker, my son ate and drank so much that it showed up after four days, and we laughed about it. We decided to take advantage of the evening dinner and night shows. I would dress up and go for dinner. My son was always there before me. This was part of our highlights and our jokes during our stay at the resort. We made sure we were on time for breakfast, lunch, and dinner. We learned how to use knives and forks by watching the other guests. We even used them to eat the fruit.

The nightly events and the breathtaking sky view made me feel peaceful and comfortable. Looking out at the ocean at night, I could see the reflection of the water glittering and dazzlingly brightly, like the stars in the sky. It was so beautiful it lit up the ocean and gave the water a shining look. It still warms my heart with such joy. The ocean's waves roared up on the edge of the rocks, splashing in and out, never stopping. The ocean never slept.

They had three cabana bars open day and night. All you could drink. I tried to enjoy it, but it did not feel right to me. I did not know how to embrace the bar-life on the ocean.

We met many people from all over the world. We exchanged phone numbers and email addresses. And even though I was on vacation, I was still prospecting. I never miss an opportunity to share a business idea, am always in a business mood, and do not know when to quit. While I was at the resort, I stayed connected with my daughter through the home security on the phone, making sure I was still monitoring the workers. While I was on the phone with my children, checking on the renovation and the contractors, I found out the workers took a break too.

It was time well spent at an all-inclusive resort in the Caribbean for two weeks. We were treated very well and took time out to visit family and friends in the towns. We did not go on any bus tours, but we loved and enjoyed our stay at the resort.

Now it was time to go home, back to our home, back to the cold, and back to the massive work ahead of us—and workers who had taken a break as soon as I left. We took the bus that picked up passengers when they arrived and took them to the resort. Now we were on the same bus going back to the airport.

We boarded our flight with no problem. But as soon as we were on the plane and took our seats, I got extremely sick. I did not know what was going on. I felt weak and dizzy; I had a runny nose. I was ready to relax, go to my bed, and be in my own space. The fun and excitement on the island took my energy, and I got sick.

I was out cold on the plane. I slept peacefully during the flight, and we arrived home on time. Not only that, I also tried to recuperate from the illness that took me over. By the time we landed, I was feeling a little better but still had a runny nose. I was grateful to be home safely. Everyone departed in an orderly fashion. We followed the crowd to where we could collect our suitcases.

As my son and I walked, we talked about our experiences on the island. My son was happy to be home. My homeland was okay except for the poverty that he saw on the streets, the condition of the old houses, the homelessness, the passion of the street vendors on the side of the streets, and the overloaded taxis packed with people. The crime and violence in the country left the people living under restrictions. What touched us the most were the workers on the Island. Especially the ones who with small children. Their wages were not enough to get them through the month, and there they had no time to get a second job. It broke my heart to see how much food was wasted at the hotel, especially since the workers could have used it for their families.

We collected our luggage and proceeded to the immigration area, where they checked our papers, as they did everyone else. They asked what we had to declare, and we declared some rum, brandy, sugarcane, and gifts for the family. One of the officers said, "Okay. Please go over there and see the customs and immigration officers."

They wanted to double-check if we were telling the truth. We complied and went to wait in line. When it was our turn, they asked us the same question again: "What do you have to declare?" I repeated my answers.

An officer asked us to open the bags, which we did. They checked our documents and one asked, "Are you permanent residents of this country?"

My son and I looked at each other in surprise. I responded, "This is my son, and he was born here. And I am a citizen."

A few officers were standing around us, so I felt pressured. But we kept calm. One of the officers asked my son, "How did you pay for your ticket for this vacation? And where do you work?" I could not believe what I was hearing. I opened my mouth and told the officer that I bought the ticket for him. Right away he said, "I am not talking to you." I felt disrespected, humiliated, and pressured by the officers. I immediately knew something was wrong. They kept trying to upset my son with question after question, just harassing him, not knowing he was under a doctor's care and on medication. He was in a discouraging situation. It felt as if we were in the right place but at the wrong time.

They kept pushing questions. They looked him up and down. Other officers came closer. When I tried to ask what the problem was, they shut me up again and said, "Please take a seat. We are not talking to you, only your son."

I was instantly shocked at the way they were talking to me. I felt like I had landed in the wrong country. "Please take a seat over there while we talk to this young man."

I could not think, tears blocked my throat, and my legs could not move. My son saw my face. He hugged me and said, "It is okay, Mom. Do as they say. Come and sit down."

Tears ran down my face. I was confused and lost. But most of all, I was afraid for my son because I knew about his health problems, and he had never been in a situation like this.

My Compass Stopped, and I Was Out of My Mind Right Away

The officers drilled him so hard. It was hard for me to sit still. I wrestled for my phone in my purse. I called my daughter and told her what was happening.

She could not understand what I was saying. It shocked her, and dismayed, she kept asking me questions I could not answer: "What happened?" "Why are they questioning him? Don't they know that he was born here?"

I was completely overwhelmed. To see my son, whom I took to my country for a two-week vacation, harassed on our return by customs and immigration officers like a pack of wolves, just like the police on the street. It blew my mind.

I went back to where they were questioning him. They tried to stop me, but I had questions for them. "This child has rights too. You must be careful how you handle him because he cannot handle pressure." I wanted to know what the problem was. But they let me know that since he was of age, they could talk to him without my consent.

This is when my son said, "Mom, Mom, they said there is a warrant out for me, and they were looking for me. They believe that the person in the picture was me!"

I almost fainted when I heard what he said. "What are they talking about? You all have the wrong person." I repeated it three times. "You are mistaken. Please check your records, officers. You have the wrong person."

Oh, they got mad at me. "Woman, sit down, and let us do our job."

My heart was beating fast, and my head started to hurt. My mouth dried up, and the tears stuck in my throat. I almost lost my mind, but I could not stop. "Please double-check your information because it is not my son on your warrant." I could not stop speaking up for my son because I could see the shock and confusion on his face.

Let me describe my son. He is very tall, about six foot two inches tall. His skin is light brown. He has a baby face and is very handsome. His walk is smooth and cool, and he is soft-spoken. My son is a black man with a serious personality and humble spirit; he is quiet and kind. He looks like a young giant, but his humility makes him a big teddy bear and our gentle giant. He is very dedicated to his family and work, and he loves and respects everyone he meets. He is helpful and caring and never argues, no matter what happens. Not only that, he also loves to read and write. He makes great rap music, which is his passion. And he does not smoke, drink, or party. He is honest, full of integrity, and always goes the extra mile. Furthermore, he looks clean and very manly.

The officers surrounded him. Some had their hands on their guns; some were in front, and some were behind him. My son stood in the middle, helpless and lost. I could not help him, so I obeyed and sat down away from them. I called my daughter again and let her know what was happening. She said, "No, Mommy, no. That cannot be! Not him, not him, they do not know he would not even take candy from a candy store."

Finally, I decided to stop worrying and think of how I could help him.

What Is the Truth, and Where Is My Faith?

From where I was sitting, I could see more officers coming together, looking, and talking as if they got a great catch! Then I remembered our family lawyer and called him right away. But there was no answer.

I waited a few minutes and then called again. He answered. I was so upset that he could not understand what I was saying. It took me a while to relate what was happening to us at the airport. He was shocked but reassured me. "Be calm. Do not worry because they have no case. But you must let them do their job. Call me when you get home."

So the lawyer could not stop them. I sat in disbelief at what was happening to my son right in front of my eyes, and I was unable to help him. This was supposed to be a simple trip, a vacation that turned into a nightmare.

While I sat there, I kept looking at my son's face. He kept telling the officers, "I do not know what you are talking about. I do not know that place, and I do not live in that area. I do not know anything." But they kept at him, so many officers talking over and over, question after question.

I jumped up again and walked over to them. "I know my child, and I am telling you all you have the wrong person. And I have called a lawyer. I will be calling the media because what you are doing is wrong."

They did not care. One of the officers said, "We are arresting your son because there is a warrant out for a person who looks like him."

Most Black Men Look Alike

All the blood left my body. My son hugged me again. "Mom, listen to me. I am innocent of this charge, and I will do as they say. You and I know they have the wrong person, but I will obey them. Please, Mom, do not cry. Just listen to them. Everything will be okay."

They took my son from me right on the spot, and I was lost and confused. My legs felt too heavy to walk. My mind was in a storm as I watched him surrounded by so many police officers with their guns on their hips, ready for anything and everything. But my son repeated, "Mom, I am innocent. Do not worry."

I cried like a baby, trying to figure out what we did wrong. I was left alone with no one to comfort me. I had six pieces of luggage to carry to meet my daughter at the arrival—without her brother. This incident took a great toll on my mind and body. My trust in the system was gone forever. They arrested my son because he looked like someone they were looking for and with no solid proof. To damage his mind and spirit right there on the spot, in the great court, without proof. They took him from the airport straight to jail, where they kept him for the weekend without bail. I went home feeling empty and defeated, and I resented taking my son on vacation because it ended so badly.

He got caught up in something he had no control over. In the end, they realized they had the wrong person and released him without ever apologizing to him or me. They made a mistake in their identity. Now I had to pick up the pieces and move on. And not complain because no one was listening. We were so grateful to have him home, and we continue to treasure every moment as a family. He did not want to sue them. We never pressured him about the awful experiences he had that weekend. This tested my faith, and I did not know how to pray. I trusted and believed someone was in control of what was happening. But then came a sudden feeling of comfort over me. I trusted God knew best. My son was stronger than I had thought. Or someone was watching over him.

I wondered if the officers were paid for the day or night they worked. I hoped they would think over the evidence or proof before they arrested the next person.

Character matters; leadership descends from character. (Rush Limbaugh)

3

PATIENCE PAYS

Being a full-time mother is one of the highest
salaried jobs; since the payment is pure love.
—Mildred B. Vermont

Do not limit your challenges;
challenge your limits.
—Jerry Dunn

We returned from the vacation in the Caribbean, and the ordeal
we encountered at the airport was over. Now back at home, I was
disappointed to see the condition of the house. It was the same as
when I left it. Not much was done. All the workers did in my absence
was to remove the old drywall and leave it bare. Old pipes and
wires are all over the place. Nothing was in place. The contractor
pretended they had to wait for this and that to start the job.

The workers took advantage of my kindness and patience. They
lied and tried to hide small mishaps from me while renovating the
home. I was having a challenging time with the contractors. They
kept changing the completion date and asking for more money. I
did not agree with the changes, and I spoke up. I insisted that they

needed to complete the renovation. Furthermore, I reminded them about the contract we agreed on and signed.

The renovation lasted until early June, three months over the set date. There were lots of mishaps and mistakes, fussing and fighting on my premises. So many difficulties just trying to get it finished the way we agreed. They cut corners. They bought cheap products and put them in my home. They were very unprofessional. But eventually, I forgave them for all the extra headaches and rude behavior in my home in front of my children. But I will never refer them to anyone or use them again.

Our family home looked so amazing that we did not want to sell or move again. We were pleased with the bright living room and the kitchen with all the new appliances. There were open concepts and pot lights all over the house, from top to bottom. New tiles, new stairs in the entire house, plus a fully renovated basement with a stand-up shower. And we added an extra room to the house. Now all was well, and the house looked brand new. It was unbelievable, and the value of the house increased for sure. I was pleased, and the children were happy with their new space.

Soon after that madness, we received an invitation from my brother to attend a wedding in June–July of that same year. The excitement in the air changed from all that we went through the past few months. We gladly accepted and started to plan for the wedding.

We had a family meeting on how we could help to accommodate other members of the family who were coming from out of town for the wedding now that we had more space. Not only that, we also needed a second car for all members of my family to get to the wedding because our small car would not fit everyone. That was not the only reason I purchased the second car. I had in mind the need to prepare my sons to get jobs and help pay bills in the future.

The wedding was wonderful and full of love. We spent time with all our family members, eating, drinking, talking, laughing, and taking lots of pictures.

A few weeks had passed since the grand wedding, and it was now back to business.

We had another family meeting, and I suggested to my sons that they get busy and do something to uplift their lives while they were still young. I set aside some of my time to listen to them every Wednesday. We would meet around the dining table at 7 p.m. We talked openly about anything that might be challenging for anyone and shared whatever helpful ideas that came up. We put together a plan to fix our credit rating and how to make extra income. We decided the boys would send out ten résumés every three months until they got jobs. And it worked.

> Do not let what you cannot do; interfere with what
> you can do. (John Wooden)

It took them a while to get into the routine, but after a few weeks, they started to work together. We started to save and not waste. I was working on myself. I joined the gym and enrolled in a massage and physio program. During all this, I went to business meetings and events to learn how to make extra income and invest. Then I started taking a course to get a life insurance license. I was grateful for all the changes in my life.

My eldest son and I gave back to the community by volunteering to help seniors with computers. At the time, I felt much better about my life and had some hope that things would get much better. But then I got sick again. I was confused, sad, and feeling discouraged.

There are no mistakes, no coincidences; all events are blessings given to us to learn from. (Elisabeth Kübler-Ross)

My mind kept wondering, *what is happening to me? How can I support my family if I keep getting sick?*

This was now the spring of 2018, and I was going backward instead of forward. And I do not know why! My legs were swollen so much I could not go to the gym anymore. Then I developed migraine headaches, and my neck and back hurt so much that I could not walk or move too fast. I ended up in the emergency room again. My children's faces were so sad to see me in that condition. I had to use a cane to walk. The doctors recommended that I take a few weeks off from all that I was doing. It was back to complete bed rest and my children taking care of me. It hurt my heart. My daughter decided that we should go to the Caribbean for the Sun Fest Festival and relax for a while. I was not sure about going to the island again, but I had never experienced the greatest, biggest music festival on the island.

Her favorite artist was performing, along with many other amazing artists. This was the right time to go for our summer vacation. We booked our flight and reserved a hotel just in case. Our first plan was to stay at some friends' place. But for some reason, they did not confirm or answer the phone, so I made other plans, and off we went. I made sure to have a backup plan. I was happy to book a hotel near the airport, just in case my friends were unable to accommodate or pick us up at the airport. My daughter, granddaughter, and I arrived on the island, and our driver from the hotel was there waiting and ready.

We got a condominium for three weeks with everything included. The rooms were small, hot, and stuffy. There were two single beds.

I could not sleep in the room. The air-conditioning was not helping; it was either too hot or too cold. The kitchen was okay. We went shopping and bought some food and snacks to get us through the first few days. We spoke to the receptionist and requested a change of room. They were kind enough to give us an upper condominium room. It was much better, and the view was so amazing. I took advantage of watching the sunset. It was a magnificent view, and I took lots of pictures of the planes as they came into land. After a few days, I contacted my friends, and they had so many stories. I just stayed at the hotel and visited them.

During our time there, we went into the town by taxi and got our groceries because it was cheaper than in the area where we were staying. The hotel had a nice pool that was cleaned every day. My granddaughter loved it and swam as often as she could. But she also liked the beaches, which were within walking distance of the hotel.

I started to get up early in the morning and go for a morning walk on the beaches. This was different for me. When I was small, I dreamed of living near the beaches, so I could swim or sit and watch the waves. The ocean and the waves were very relaxing for me.

We met a few people wherever we went. I was surprised by how friendly the locals were to me. On weekdays we visited family, and on the weekend, we went to Sun Fest 2018.

My daughter felt sick, and we were very worried about her condition. She was not eating much and complained about stomach pains and dizziness. I thought she had to eat something at the festival, which got her so sick. I wanted to cut the vacation short. What was more important now was her health. We had a few days left, which we spent at the hotel. She slept most of the day while I watched TV, wrote, and played with my granddaughter. My granddaughter and

I went to the store, and she went swimming in the pool. There were few children around that hotel, so she about had the pool to herself.

My daughter started to look pale, and I felt the need to bring her to a local clinic. But she refused to go. After a few days of morning sickness, she told us she thought that she was pregnant. I was shocked and surprised but still happy for her. I had one granddaughter and thought, we *hoped this baby will be a boy*. I was a grandmother at an early age, long before my oldest sibling. There were so many mixed emotions that day. I felt pleased to welcome another member to our family. She was not ready to have more babies because her oldest was ten years older. She had given up on having more babies, but I had not. We hugged, cried, laughed, and enjoyed the rest of our trip.

Besides, I knew God had a purpose for our lives.

After two weeks and four days had passed, we were ready to go home. We went into town and did some shopping, including gifts for family and friends. We woke up the next day excited and ready to go home. We did the last-minute packing of our clothes, toothbrushes, and sleeping clothes and went to the airport as scheduled. We were early for our flight, but we planned it that way. We checked our luggage at customs to free our hands and walked around the airport to see the beautiful souvenir shops and liquor stores, and to get a last taste of Caribbean food. We exchanged our currency, went on the plane, and headed home.

4

MY FAITH HAS BEEN TESTED

A mind is like a parachute. It does
not work if it is not open.
—Frank Zappa

After months and months of uncertainty about my identity and after several attempts to get my old passport renewed, I found out that my birth certificate was not valid. It did not make sense to me. I never experienced such uncertainty and emptiness until then. I was hoping to go home as a returning resident. Not only that, I needed to get a new passport, but how to approach this situation was more than I expected. Where do you go and what do you do after finding out that your birth papers are not valid? I asked the Creator for his help and left the idea alone. Furthermore, I decided to have another meeting with the children, this time to inform them about my birth papers.

The greatest news was the new addition to our family. My daughter was pregnant at the time, and I was incredibly happy for her. At the end of February, my daughter had another baby girl, and I was in the delivery room. I cut the umbilical cord of the second grandchild.

All went well, and she came home from the hospital with the new baby in two days. I was profoundly grateful. But a few days after delivery, her legs and both breasts started to swell and were painful. She was also running a fever. She was having a demanding time nursing the baby at first and got little or no sleep day or night. I did not know what to do. I hoped and prayed for her to be okay. We did not go to the doctor. Instead, I tried cold and hot compresses for days until she got some relief. We used the back of a comb to comb her breast to help with circulation in her breast, and it worked.

Weeks later, the baby and mother were doing very well. I was grateful to God for his help. I never fully understood what happened to her. I just trusted him.

The room she occupied before the baby was now too small. I switched rooms and gave them my room, the master bedroom. I now lived in the smallest room in the five-bedroom house. But I was grateful and humble. All I needed was a bed, a desk, and my computer. A space to read my books on how to become the best me and financially fit. I read book after book. I visited the library to borrow books and read them. If I found them valuable enough, I bought them on Amazon and then passed them on to my sons and daughter.

I encouraged them to read books that would inspire them to broaden their horizons and improve their knowledge and wisdom. I encouraged them to read the Bible. I insisted—and still insist—that godly wisdom is especially important and will change their lives.

During the early fall and winter of 2018–2019, the weather was getting cold, and I constantly felt depressed and full of doubts. Even though I was reading many books on self-development and filled with inspirational ideas, I still needed to learn how to relax. I was working on myself mentally and physically. But I needed to go somewhere I would not be tempted to do anything but rest. I decided it would be a great idea to take some time for myself and go to the Caribbean for a few months.

This was also my chance to learn how to renew the birth papers that I was applying for at the head office, but they could not find the information. My blood pressure was going up instead of down. I was under doctors' care, so no work or housework. That was ridiculously hard for me because I love my surroundings to be always clean. The house was fully renovated from top to bottom, and the mortgage, debts, credit cards, and bills are up to date. The children were safe and comfortable. We installed a security system in the home so whenever I decided to travel, I could still monitor the children and the home from my iPhone. All was well.

This was my opportunity to visit my homeland by myself. While I was planning, the news out of my homeland was not good. There were reports that most returning residents faced home robberies or burglaries. Some were murdered by strangers or family members. All over the news and social media were stories every week about incidents of brutal violence, murders, and other crimes happening to some returning resident. My children were worried about my safety since I was planning to be there for a few months.

As a Returning Resident, You Have Been Warned

I had no fear of traveling to my homeland. I had nowhere else to go, and I felt that all would be okay with me on the island. Though I felt confident and open to going, my children were not happy about my decision to go. I did not talk about it anymore. Not only that, but I also packed my suitcases quietly and called a few travel agents to see what was available for the end of the year. And I waited.

Somehow the last few weeks and days the time seemed shorter, lonely, and challenging. The days were going so fast. I reviewed my responsibilities to make sure I left no stone unturned and hoped for the best. Every day there was one unwelcome news story after another. It was a moment in time to see if I was ready for what was ahead of me.

October was my granddaughter's birthday, and I spent time with her. Then November was my birthday month, and I got some unwelcome news that someone I admired suddenly passed. I felt sad, and it made me think about what I needed to do.

My faith has truly been tested. His death left me feeling unsure about life. No one knew the day or time of death. My children were so supportive and loving. They bought gifts for my birthday. I thank them for being so thoughtful.

The next month was December and Christmas. We had dinner at home as a family. My faith had been tested in every area of my life, but I stayed calm. I kept saying to myself, "Keep a cool head, no matter what happens. If the children see you worried, they will be worried too."

The next day I woke up feeling ready and sure that this was my time to move. I picked up the phone and called the travel agent to book my ticket to go to the Caribbean for three months.

I also called a dear friend and asked permission to stay at his house on the island. He responded, "You are like family. Anytime you are ready." It was okay with him, and he would send his driver to pick me up at the airport.

I was now mentally ready to go to my homeland. My ticket was booked for a flight on December 31, 2019, and I had been packed for months; I believed for one year. When I told my children, they were shocked to see that I had made up my mind to go now or never to the island.

I gave my two sons instructions about what was expected from them to maintain the newly renovated home. I love and trust them.

My daughter said, "Mom, I am going with you." I was not sure what to say because she was very persistent that I should not go alone. She booked tickets for herself and her children, and I invited my youngest son to travel with me the same day. They planned to spend three weeks; I was staying for three months.

Great, great, I am finally going to the Caribbean as a returning resident. Out of the snow and ready to soak up the sun. Yes, I was excited and free from what I left behind and was faithfully looking ahead. I had been using a cane to walk for the last few months. Now I parked the cane in the closet and walked in faith. Not only that, but I also stepped into faith, and faith carried me to my homeland mentally ready.

> Obstacles are things a person sees when he takes his eyes off his goal. (E. Joseph Cossman)

5

MY HOMELAND: PAST, PRESENT, AND NOW

We landed on the island on December 31, 2019, and the driver of my dear friend picked us up on time. Everything looked so different to me because my mindset was ready to learn about my culture for the first time.

We stopped at a huge supermarket and exchanged our money for island currency. We bought bottles of water and some snacks for the children just until we settled in to do a big shopping trip.

We went to my friend's mansion. We had private courts away from anyone else. There was a huge bedroom with two queen beds. A shower and an outdoor kitchen were ready for our use only. The place was fully walled and had a solid gate; no one could enter without permission from the boss. We felt safe, at peace, and full of joy. The place was nice and clean, a perfect little space for me to stay in for the next three months. I rented a car for a few days. This was my first time driving on the island, but I was not scared to drive. I was noticeably confident and brave. Besides, I needed to overcome all my fears now or never.

During our first week, we drove to the city and did our shopping. We bought enough food to last us at least two weeks. We wanted to go to the beach and rivers near the place where we were staying, but it did not work out for us. Likewise, we looked around until we found the best white sand beaches and rivers. We spent most of our days at the river.

Roaring River Is a Wonderful Tourist Area

We had a dedicated service for the baby at the river because we thought it was the right thing to do. Afterward, we had to rededicate the baby because it was not biblical. It was beautiful to just relax. I recalled going to this place once with my dad. The local people were welcoming and kind, nothing like what we were hearing on the news and social media. We spent most of our time just relaxing at the river.

I only rented the car when we needed to go far. Once in the area, we used the local taxi to get around.

I had some personal unfinished business that I started while I was in a foreign country, and officials there suggested it would be best to go to the Caribbean and get it done. I needed to get it done before my vacation time ran out. One day I went to the city by myself to inquire about renewing my birth certificate. It was a small office that dealt with birth and death registries. Many people were lined up outside before it even opened.

The waiting time was long. I kept cool until it was my turn. I was informed that it would take a few weeks to get such information, and it would cost me some money. I was grateful and hopeful. I paid for their services and got my receipts. I went back to where I was staying and waited for a call.

I kept myself remarkably busy in order not to worry about my birth papers. I planned events with my children. We visited many places so I could share my culture with them. We would cook food, pack our bags with all we needed for lunch, and go to the river for the day. In the evening, we would relax at the mansion, listen to music, and talk about the day. The children loved sitting on their phones while I read my books.

We were happy with the place we were staying in and the people in the area. I did not feel threatened or scared to walk on the streets or take the local taxis. My youngest son, daughter, new baby, and granddaughter were enjoying themselves on the island. When we were in the big city, we did not see any violence or any crime like what we saw and heard about on the news. I wondered if the news was real or propaganda.

I did not get a callback from the register office. It had been two weeks since I applied to renew my birth papers. Not only that, but I also called on Monday morning and spoke to a lady. I gave her the file number. She put me on hold for a minute, and when she returned, she said, "They need more time to search for the original copy. Call back in a week." I said okay and hung up the phone, feeling strange and a little lost.

It was nearing time for the children to go home. I took them shopping in the city again. When I was parking, I had an accident, damaging the front of the car. I was a little shocked. I did not hit another person. I stayed calm and focused because I did not want to scare the children. Likewise, I told the owner of the vehicle, and he was cool. I had to pay for the repairs.

We spent the rest of the week washing, packing, and preparing them for their flight. I told them to eat, drink, and smoke all they wanted because they could not take it with them. The owner of the car and I dropped the children off at the airport. I hugged and kissed them and made sure they got on their flight. Then I went back to the West to start my vacation by myself.

6

PROOF OF EXISTENCE

What man is he that desireth life; and
loveth many days, that he may see good?
—Psalm 34:12

The first week of February 2020 came and still no response from the register office regarding my birth certificate papers. I prepared to go to the office in person to speak to someone and get my old passport renewed all at once. I felt confident and hopeful that I would get through today. Not only that, but I also paid for the search weeks ago. There had been more than enough time for a simple search.

I reached the office early and was the second person in the waiting area. I took a ticket and sat and waited. One hour passed, two hours. Then I wondered, *what is taking so long?* I went to ask the receptionist when I could speak to someone regarding my birth papers. She said, "Just wait awhile. They will call you soon."

I went back to my seat. I felt thirsty, tired, and frustrated. Plus, it was getting busy and hot inside the small waiting area as people started to fill up the spaces. Families with small children were there too. I finally went outside to get fresh air and cool down.

After four hours of waiting, they called my number. The lady said to me, "Take a seat. Do you have your old birth certificate and passport?"

"Yes, Miss," I replied in excitement, I gave her the papers right away. As she looked at them, I sat with an empty feeling in my stomach, holding my excitement within. I wondered, *what is taking them so long just to find a piece of paper?*

She walked away, and when she returned, she said, "Please go over to that office, and that lady will assist you." I felt a bit confused, but I went to the next lady who was sitting in the tiny office.

She was pleasant and professional. She said, "Please have a seat, Miss. I need to go over your documents to verify your identification."

Now I felt that I had been shuffled from one person to the next. She started to ask lots of questions, things I could not fully comprehend. But I did my best because it was about me. She asked about my parents, my siblings, and my status as a citizen. I felt as if I did something wrong by applying for a new birth certificate so I could renew my passport.

She worked on her computer for about five minutes—it seemed like ten minutes to me—without saying a word. I was getting nervous. Many thoughts rushed into my mind, and I felt dizzy. *What is the problem? Why are they investigating me? Is this how they renew people's documents?*

I took a deep breath and released it slowly. Finally, she said, "Miss, I do not know how to explain this matter, but your document has been changed. We are unable to find your name or existence in our system."

My heart stopped for a second. "What, what do you mean? You cannot find me in your system, and my document is changed? Changed how? I have my old passport here with me." I showed it to her.

"The number on the top right-hand corner of your birth paper has been changed and doesn't match the person by this name."

I was flabbergasted, and my mouth gaped wide open. Not only that I was shocked by the news, but I also suddenly felt a sharp pain in my chest, and there were tears in my eyes. I could not move from my seat. Then I asked, "Are you sure they did not make a mistake? Miss, what can I do?" She was kind and patiently tried to explain that it was a mistake and that I could apply for a deeper search. It would cost me much more money, but sometimes missing documents showed up during the search.

With a glimmer of hope, I controlled my emotions and asked, "What do I need to do?" She suggested that I get the money together then come back to the office and ask for a deep search. They would send the information to all the register offices on the island. I walked out of the office like a snail, sad, broken, and out of my mind. My high hopes and spirit were crushed.

All that was playing in my head was, *I have no proof of existence. Mi,* no exist. How is that? How can this be? This must be a big mistake. Mi, no exist!

I kept walking and talking to myself aloud. Then I laughed and shook my head. No, man, this is a joke. Who is playing with me? I took the local van back to Westmoreland. I sat so quietly on the bus; I could hear everyone talking and laughing. But I sat still because my mind was shocked by the news. I was alone at a time when I did not want to be alone. And for some reason, things seemed so different. I grieved for a few days, sad and lost for words. Furthermore, I could not explain what was happening to me. All that kept playing in my mind was, *we cannot find any person by that name.*

It took me a week to gather my thoughts before I reached out and talked to my daughter. She said, "Mom, how are you doing? You sound different from the last time we spoke. Are you okay?"

"Well, my daughter, I am a little beside myself right now. I tried to renew the birth papers and passport, but I could not get it done?"

"What is the problem? Do you need money?"

"No, no. They cannot find me in their system."

"What? What are you talking about, Mom?"

"I went to the registry office and spoke to one of the receptionists. They have no registry of me. They cannot find it. I do not exist in their system." I started to cry again. She was so upset because she knew I was in the Caribbean all by myself. Every day she called, and we talked about what to do next and how to deal with this matter. She suggested that I call my mother and ask if she could help.

My mother was shocked and could not believe the news. "That is not possible," she said. "It must be there."

I went back to the registry office and paid the extra money for the deep search. Now the game began. They gave me some papers to complete and return with information about each member of my family.

I now had homework to do. I had to call each member of my family; some of them I had not spoken to for years. I explained why I needed this information over and over. It felt like I was reliving a nightmare with everyone saying the same thing, "It's impossible." It took me a week going back and forth with my siblings before I was able to complete the papers.

My mother was not pleased with what I was dealing with and asked me, "Why are you worrying about your old passport paper? Aren't you already a permanent citizen?" That got my mind instantly in a whirlwind. My identity is part of me, and my birth papers and passport speak volumes, dead or alive.

I could not wrap my mind around the way she was thinking. I let it go and continued searching for my proof of existence. I finished the application, paid the extra fees, and asked when I would hear from them again. I was told that it sometimes took six weeks, six months, or even a year.

I did not want to talk about it anymore because it only made me depressed. I decided to put it aside and do something else with my time. It has now been three years, and I still have not received any response or confirmation on the birth papers.

> You are never a loser until you quit trying. (Mike Ditka)

7

RASTA OR ROOTS

Although no one can go back and make
a brand-new start, anyone can start from
now and make a brand-new ending.
                                   —Carl Bard

Rasta was a big part of my identity, and my locks have been very secret to me since I was a young adult. I get my strength from my locks. It is my beauty, and I feel confident and brave with it even though I have been treated very badly because of the color of my skin and my locks. But I never let that stop me from standing up for righteousness and truth.

Rasta represents some parts of my culture, the ancient ones, and my ancestors that I never knew. I grew up listening to reggae/roots music and watching my parents express their love to everyone. I loved their humility and kindness toward the poor.

I became a Rasta back in the early nineties. No one wants to associate themselves with Rastas, ganja, or anyone who was a part of that group. Not everyone who has locks smokes. My locks were a key representation of my Rasta habits and roots music. I embraced the Rastafarian culture. My children and I faced massive discrimination because of our locks and the blackness of my skin. But I never let that stop me from going to school and working. Now, in the twenty-first century, Rasta is fully accepted in the world forum.

From the forties to the sixties, roots were the in thing, and I lived by it. I consider myself old school with a Rasta twist. I am seeking to know the truth of my origin in this world. My roots, as I was told, are in the history books going back as far as 1655 and 1867. My paternal grandmother was a Maroon. She had a very dark complexion and lived by the spirit of truth. She had a beautiful spirit with an unspeakable love for all humankind.

The Maroons were descendants of the Africans. They freed themselves from slavery in the colony of Jamaica, where I was born. They were enslaved Africans who worked on sugarcane plantations. When the slaves freed themselves, they became Maroons. This caused the crash of the sugarcane economy in Jamaica. The Maroons were considered freemen. Jamaica became a Crown colony in 1866, and by 1962, they got their independence. Their motto is, "Out of many, we are one people."

Maroons have migrated in many parts of the world. I learned that they were Maroons in Nova Scotia, one of Canada's thirteen provinces. They are also in the Bahamas and Gambia. The Sierra Leone settlers and African Americans were the founders of Freetown on March 11, 1792, after the American Revolutionary War.

> Any Rasta will tell you that Rastafarian beginnings are not in Jamaica, but Africa. All of Africa symbolizes a homeland, and holy land, to the Rastafarians. Their roots are African. (Tracy Nicholas/Bill Sparro)

In 1934, there were groups of men who believed that His Imperial Majesty was the living God. They preached this to the people in the streets of Kingston, Jamaica. They developed a love for the emperor because of the great oppression they were facing. During that time, they looked to Africa for support, and the emperor's life was just forming. They revered and accepted him as the coming messiah. Back then, street preachers used the Bible to prophesy that he was the king of kings and the lord of lords. At the time, I do not believe most people were able to read the Bible for themselves; they were misinformed. There is only one leader, and that is the Holy Spirit. And he is the correct way to the Holy One of Israel.

Over the years, Marcus Garvey saw the potential in the emperor and said, "Look to the East for the coming of a black King." L. P. Howell and many others spread this doctrine, and people took comfort in it. But there is only one comforter, the Holy Spirit.

In 1935, the *Jamaica Times* published accounts of the activities of the Nyabinghi Order of Warriors in Ethiopia. Reportedly led by His Imperial Majesty Haile Selassie I, the Nyabingi Order sought to achieve the overthrow of white domination by racial war. In Jamaica, "Niyabinghi" came to be called "Niya men." The idea of violence as a tool for freedom spread like wildfire, and in 1935 and1936, all leaders associated with the movement were repeatedly arrested on suspicion of rebelliousness" (Nicholas and Sparro, *Rastafari: A Way of Life,* p. 24).

Many songs are well-played in the music industry, but I choose to highlight this one. This is a song that inspires people to be Rasta without the locks. But I do not believe the people recognized the lyrics: "You don't have to be dread to be Rasta, It's the conception of the heart." That's a true statement. You do not have to be dread to be Rasta. But our hearts belong to the Creator. Who should we give praise to?

If your heart is not for Yah, the Might Creator of heaven and earth, then it is worshipping false gods and following false doctrine. What is the first commandment of the Highest? And what do you value in this life? Can a man give you the breath of life or inner peace?

How would people know the lie from the truth? They were not taught; they were told. Since they listened to the ones who were outspoken and well-read, they believed anything they heard.

> And many false prophets shall rise and shall deceive many. (Matt. 24:11; 24:24)

> My people are destroyed for lack of knowledge; because thou hast rejected knowledge, I will also reject thee, that thou shalt be no priest to me: seeing thou hast forgotten the law of thy God, I will also forget thy children. (Hos. 4:6)

> And the times of this ignorance God winked at, but now commandeth all men everywhere to Repent. (Acts 17:30–31)

"Roots" means foundation. I am rooted in truth and righteousness. I hate evil and lies. Not only that, but I also cannot stand to see wickedness of any sort. That is my roots. Furthermore, I am willing to do all I can to always stay on the right path. My parents were a roots couple. They stuck together through thick and thin and raised six children.

Their love and care for us are what nurtured me to love roots living. They did not attend church, but they sent us to church. They did not know that some of the churches that followed the Catholic system were brainwashing systems. Their system was implemented between the fifteenth and eighteenth centuries, when the Jesuits traveled to the four corners of the world and planted the missionaries that led to evangelization and apostolic ministry in 112 nations. These were the early globalizers who modernized the world. Do we find God—Yah—in the churches or ourselves?

Following are some quotes from leaders throughout history that I used in my life to remind me to fix my moral compass before I tried to fix others:

> God and nature first made us what we are, and then out of our own created genius we make ourselves what we want to be. Follow always that great law. Let the sky and God be our limit and Eternity our measurement. (Marcus Garvey)

> Liberate the minds of men, and ultimately you will liberate the bodies of men. (Marcus Garvey)

> I am not African because I was born in Africa, but because Africa was born in me. (Kwane Nkrumah)

> We need more light about each other. Light creates understanding, understanding creates love, love creates patience and patience creates unity. (Malcolm X)

The Bible is full of proof of life. The book of Genesis has many biblical stories, but the one I find interesting is the creation story. The Adam and Eve story can be defined only through godly wisdom with spiritual eyes and ears. The story is about giants on the earth and is a great mystery. I am from the seed of Abraham, which is one of our ancestors, and Isaac and Jacob.

> Remember Abraham, Isaac, and Israel, thy servants to whom thou swarest, and saidst unto them, I will

multiply your seed as the stars of heaven, and all this land that I have spoken of will I give unto your seed, and they shall inherit it forever. (Ex. 32:13)

God cannot lie.

Now, to Abraham and his seed were the promises made. He saith not, and to seeds, as of many: but as of one, and to thy seed, which is The Messiah. (Gal. 3:16)

Any roots that are pure and true will last long only if their groundation and foundation are rooted in righteousness and truth. "Yah is the way, the truth and the life." (John 14:6)

But now, O LORD, thou art our Father; We are the clay; and thou our potter; and we all are the work of thy hand. (Isa. 64:8)

What more proof do we need? In whose hand is the soul of every living thing, and the breath of all mankind. (Job 12:10)

I am the vine; you are the branches. If you remain in me and I in you, you will bear much fruit; apart from me, you can do nothing. (John 15:5)

What then? Are we better than they are? No. Everyone will fall from grace if they do not worship the true and living God in this life.

I consider myself a child of God, and that is where my roots begin and end.

8

DRIVEN BY A FORCE: NO LOOKING BACK

Over the years, I read lots of self-development books and attended seminars. But nothing prepared me for this moment.

I was on the island alone for the first time. I was not afraid, lonely, or sad even though my family was not there with me. I sought the Bible to find ways to inspire myself. I found the Bible more inspiring than all the books I brought to read. I still read my Bible more often than my other books. At that time, something about the Bible was calling me to it. I felt so comfortable after reading the Bible. I started to write down some verses I liked. I thought about the words and what they meant. Not only that, but I also wrote my thoughts in the notes section of my IPhone.

I wrote some poems and read them aloud to myself. I played music, cooked, ate food, and smoked to relax. I wondered; *how can I learn about the Creator? Does he think about me, what I am here for?* I read the Bible and started to seek him. How could I know him? I heard other people say, "He is a friend and Father." Lots of questions keep popping up in my mind. I wrote them down and reread and answered them using the scriptures in the Bible. I was amazed to see the Word jumping at me. I started to read for hours without even knowing that I did not eat. Rather, I was feeding on the words in the Bible.

I set a schedule to wake up before sunrise and read my Bible for four hours. Before I went to bed, I read for two hours and then went to bed early, as early as nine o'clock. I kept focused. I did not know how to pray, but I knew how to read. I read more and listened to the radio. Furthermore, I did not watch TV or fancy videos. I read other books and wrote for an hour every day because I did not need to go anywhere. I started to study the Bible more and ask myself questions:

> What is my purpose here?
> What can I do to help others?
> How can I give back to my community?

That is when my mindset started to change. I felt a new light of hope in my life.

In 2019, stories about violence in schools were broadcast on the island. The students were fighting each other and their teachers. The everyday news and radio reports were displeasing to my ears. I wondered, *why is this happening to the teachers and students? How can I be of help to them?*

Something very strange was happening with this generation, something I could not believe. During my time as a student in my homeland, we had such respect for our teachers that we would never talk back to our teachers, much less fight them.

Did I feel eager to give to my community? Would it help if I shared my life experience with the students?

Those were some of the questions I wrote in the back of my mind. I was neither a motivational speaker nor famous. Would they listen to this poor girl from abroad? I wanted to reach out to the children because it broke my heart to hear about the division between teachers and students. But I did not know how to do it.

I decided to visit a friend, Mrs. Blake, who lived in the town. I had not seen or spoken to her for years. I had traveled for months but never got the chance to visit. But I stepped out in faith, not sure if she still lived there, and I had no phone number for her. I went into the town and took a taxi to go to the last place I knew she lived. I sat in the front seat to make sure I could see where I needed to get off.

It was a long ride to my friend's house. The area looked different; there were newly developed homes and paved streets. It looked amazing. After a while, I saw an area I remembered. "Do you know the Blake family?" I asked the driver. He said yes, which made me so happy. He dropped me off right in front of their gate. I paid him and got out of the taxi.

I looked at the house, which looked bigger than what I recalled. I took a deep breath. *Well, I have reached this far and cannot turn back now,* I thought, and walked up to the gate. It was closed and fully chained up. There was a car in the driveway. *Great. Someone must be home.* I called out her name: "Mrs. Blake. Mrs. Blake." There was no answer. I stood there wondering, *Is this the right place, or did they sell their house and move after their son died?* Their son was my dear friend. He died in a car accident at a young age.

I yelled again, "Mrs. Blake, Mrs. Blake, it's me." Still no answer. I kept wondering if it was a good idea to show up without notice or invitation. I looked around and saw a neighbor who looked out to see who was yelling. I smiled and asked if Mrs. and Mr. Blake were living here. She said, "Yes, but you must keep calling. She will hear you eventually."

With great excitement, I called out more loudly, "Mrs. Blake, Mrs. Blake."

I heard a lady's voice call out, "Oh, who is that?"

"Mrs. Blake, it's me, your friend from abroad."

"From abroad? Wait a minute." She looked and said, "Oh my! I cannot believe it is you."

"Yes, Mrs. Blake. It is me!" She was so excited to see me that she hurried to the gate, forgetting she needed the keys to open it. I was driven by a force beyond my understanding. I found the Blakes, thank God. Yes, I stepped out in faith and found the Blake family after many years.

It was like I won a jackpot because it had been so long since I had seen her, and I was grateful to have been a friend of their dearly departed son. She returned with the keys after about five minutes and opened the gate. We laughed with joy to see each other. I said, "You're chained up good." We embraced each other so tightly. We laughed, hugged, and cried for joy. "It is so wonderful to finally see you. And I am so glad you did not move." Thank God, thank God.

She shouted out with joy to her husband, "We have a visitor, honey, and it's a person from abroad."

We walked up some stairs leading to the rooftop of their house. Mr. Blake was sitting in a chair with a big smile on his face. I went over and hugged him. He said, "My friend, my friend, it has been so long. Where have you been?"

I was lost for words, too overwhelmed to express what life had done to and for me. I wanted to tell him I was afraid to visit because of the memories of his son's death. His death left me so sad, and that was why I stayed away. So much was going on in my mind, but I said nothing. I sat down with Mr. Blake while Mrs. Blake went to make lunch. "How are you doing?" I asked. "It is good to see you. How is life treating you?"

"I had a stroke after my son's death. I am unable to walk or help myself now. My wife has been doing everything for me. It is hard."

Mrs. Blake came back with a big smile on her face and lunch in her hand. I thanked her, and we all ate and talked about joyful things. She was so grateful to see me. She asked me where I was staying and how I found them. I explained that I had walked out in faith, and I found them.

After a few hours of sad but joyful moments, I told them I had to head back before nightfall to where I was staying in the countryside. They invited me to come back and spend some time with them before I returned home. I agreed, but I would call before visiting them. She gave me the house and cell numbers and then walked me to get a taxi. We talked for a bit. My heart ached to see Mr. Blake was in that condition, but she said, "All we can do is pray for him."

The taxi came, and she made sure I was inside before she returned to her home. I hugged her goodbye, entered the taxi, and waved bye. A wonderful lady and I was pleased with the way she always welcomed me into her family.

9

STARVING FOR RIGHTEOUSNESS

On the way back to the countryside, I had mixed feelings about Mr. Blake's condition and his son's death. I tried to stay focused on the road until I reached the town. From town, I still had to walk quite a distance to get a bus to the countryside, so I kept moving, deep in thought, and not stopping to talk to anyone.

When I reached my destination, I sat down for a second to think about what an interesting day it was. I could have jumped for joy having found the Blake family after not seeing or hearing from them for almost fifteen years. Mission accomplished. I was pleased with myself, so I got something to eat and drink. Then built a splif to smoke. But for some reason, the smoke did not taste so good anymore.

I grabbed my Bible, sat down, and started to read. I read until nightfall, but I could not get enough. I turned on the light and kept reading. Not only that, but I was starving for the right way to approach life.

Furthermore, I was alone, with no one to distract me. It felt right. I read until bedtime. I closed the front gate to the apartment and went inside my room, took a shower, and went to bed.

And the work of righteousness shall be peace; and
the effect of righteousness quietness and assurance
forever. (Isa. 32:17)

I woke up early the next morning, ready to read the Bible again. I
had other books to read and was working on a manuscript, but the
Bible was so attractive and compelling that I could not get enough
of it. But I knew I had to finish my manuscript and get the book
ready for the editor and publishing company.

All my thoughts were on finding the right way of living. I started
to write down Bible verses I liked. I also made notes of verses that I
heard and read them in the Bible. My notepad was full of questions,
but I had no one to whom I could pose them. I stayed grounded
for about two weeks, just reading and reciting Bible verses. I found
a radio station that had morning prayers, and I listened to some
pastors preaching and praying. I wondered, *Can I learn to pray like
him or remember the Bible verses to say them as he did?*

During those two weeks, I thought about Mr. Blake and his
condition. I recalled that my children's father had a stroke too. I
needed to go and spend at least a weekend with the Blake family.
I had no clue what I would talk about with them, but it touched
my heart to see him so sick. I did some research on what causes a
stroke and how to use natural medicine to help someone. There were
several verses in the Bible about how we can support each other by
encouraging each other. Something in the Bible was talking to my
spirit, but I did not yet understand how to respond.

I began to search the Bible, books, and radio stations for the Word
of God. I recalled playing the song "Be Still" by the recording artist
Akae Beka. I played it over and over, trying to understand what it
meant.

I was overwhelmed with compassion for others and the obstacles they were facing in their lives. I started to remember all the challenging years I went through with no one to talk with about all the disappointments, especially those caused by people I thought were there for me. All my pain and hurt, and the unforgiving mindset that I was dealing with. I could not understand how to overcome them. I got a burst of energy to do a massive cleanup and change my room around. I put most of my clothes in a bag. I thought about who I could give some clothes and shoes to. I realized I did not have enough dresses, so I decided to go into town wearing pants and buy long skirts and dresses. I always covered my hair with a scarf, but I did not feel right wearing short skirts and pants. I now felt so convinced to dress more modestly.

I was thirsting for something that money could not buy, or humankind could not give. I did not care about becoming famous or popular. I loved myself just as I was. I never had desires for accolades or fame; those things were far from my mind. I was fully accomplished. Money was not my problem. I knew how to make money. I finished high school, went to college, and worked for fourteen years in the health field. I was married three times, had my children and grandchildren, and bought a home. I was a co-author of two books that is on Amazon and was now working on three books. There will be more books in the future. I had the opportunity to be an extra in two movie productions and to travel a bit. I was not shy. I chose to be single and walk in faith, just starving for righteousness.

My thirst led me to the Bible. The more I read, the more I saw that I needed to change my moral compass to fit the Holy Spirit's will and find a way for my life. No more my way.

I kept reading the Bible every day. I hoped to find some people with whom I could read and share what I was learning. On the weekend, especially Sundays, I reached out to people in the neighborhood.

I would see people walking to church, but I did not know how to express what I was going through or even how to ask them if I could attend their church just to learn about the Redeemer. I did not know how to approach them because I had my locks, and some people thought a person with locks only smoke ganja and were not interesting in the Bible or believe in the Savior.

There I was, stuck in the middle of culture and traditions. Am I Rasta, roots, or a Christian? And I did not know what to do. *I have utterly lost my identity*, I thought.

I was not an island girl or a foreigner.
I was not a Christian or a Rasta, so who am I?

I dug deep into the books, especially the Bible, for my identity. I needed to know which direction I should go to find the truth about who I am, why I am here, and where to go.

I used the Bible as my stepping stone to gaining wisdom and understanding. I needed freedom from outside distractions. I devoted myself to studying the Bible every day. Nothing was more important to me than my newfound love, the Bible.

The radio talked about Saturday worship and Sunday worship, but I did not understand either. The word "church" was a taboo word because people go there to learn how to stop sinning. Some backslid, and some never changed. They went back out into the world and lived the same as they had before, or even worse. The church does not change the person, only the Holy Spirit. Could the Holy Spirit only be found in the churches?

I kept looking for answers in the Bible and still listened to the song "Be Still." I decided to search for what he meant by the saying, "Be still." I looked for all the biblical verses that said to "be still." I was shocked at the meaning.

"Be still, and know that I am God: I will be exalted among the heathen, I will be exalted in the earth" (Psalm 46:10). To be still, one must become disciplined and as obedient to Yah as his disciples. I wanted to know more about how to keep still, not stiff, and still alive.

I decided to visit the Blake family, but now I was ready to share the Word of God with them. After doing some research on the best verse, I was ready to share it with Mr. Blake and inspire him to pray and praise God for the grace and mercy to heal him. I called Mrs. Blake and let her know I was available to visit for the weekend. I packed my bag with some clothes and my laptop. I took a minivan from the countryside to the city and then transferred to the local taxi to their home. I knew exactly where I was going now.

There were a few people in the taxi. The driver was driving fast and playing music very loudly. No one dared tell him to lower the volume or to slow down. I humbled myself in the front because I was a foreigner, and I wondered if once I talked, he might charge me more money. He drove down the main road, overtaking trucks, and other cars. I prayed in my heart to reach the Blakes' safely. Soon after, he reached the area, and it was such a relief. I got out of the taxi, paid him, and walked off.

I reached the house of the Blake family and called out to Mrs. Blake. She immediately came to open the gate and gave me a warm welcome. She gave me a room to myself. I put my stuff in the room and then went upstairs and sat with Mr. Blake. We talked for hours. I introduced what I had in mind to do with him in the morning, and he was happy.

Self-Righteousness Is Not Righteousness

I said good night and went to my room, so excited about being in their company.

When I awoke the next morning, I took a shower and got ready to share my morning devotion with them. Mr. and Mrs. Blake were the first people I ever shared the Bible with. We sat down and read some verses. I explained the verses to them. Mrs. Blake was surprised to see and hear me reciting the Bible. She asked me, "Where did you learn to relate the verses to us so well?"

"I have been studying the Bible since I arrived on the island. I wanted to share it with anyone willing and open to listening, but I found no one." I chose to share it with them because I believed it would help her husband to recover if he believed in and trusted God. I told her I was hoping to give back to the children in the school, especially in my community.

Suddenly, she mentioned that her daughter was a teacher, and she could ask her to allow me to visit her classroom to speak to the students who were about to graduate. This was the opportunity of a lifetime for me. Giving back to the youth or others on the island became the highlight of my trip. I always dreamed that it would be great to visit and do something for my country and community.

This felt right to my spirit, and it happened. My starving for righteousness was finally working out for the good of all.

> And he believed in the Lord, and he counted it to him for righteousness. (Gen.15:6)

He that walketh uprightly, and worketh righteousness and speaketh the truth in his heart. (Ps. 15:2)

Do not be afraid to ask dumb questions. They are easier to handle than dumb mistakes. (Carolyn Coats)

10

GIVING BACK

I was so excited about Mrs. Blake's offer. She made all the arrangements for me to get to that school. In the morning, I went with a student who lived in the area to the school and spoke to a class of students ready to graduate.

This was my first time in front of a classroom of students and sharing my experience with them. I was more excited to share than nervous. I talked for about an hour, and they sat and listened. The teacher agreed with me and asked me to please repeat: "I told them if they do not obey the ones who are caring for them now, how can they look forward to going out in this world and living a successful life?"

I told the class that I had not correctly used the opportunity I received as a teenager when I went abroad. I did not understand what opportunity meant. Not only that, but I also lived a reckless life. I ran away from home at fourteen years old and was homeless with other runaway children. We drank and smoked because we thought that would make us cool. I did not go to school. I thought my mother was too strict, so I became very rebellious to her rules. And I paid a hefty price for my immoral behavior.

By the time I was sixteen, I was in jail for stealing and fighting. At eighteen, I was shot in the face for trying to stop a domestic dispute. But that did not stop me. I went on and on, living carefree and foolishly for years, even after I became a single parent of two. I used drugs and drank and partied a lot.

I also became a drug dealer and one of the top smugglers. I trained other girls in how to make money. Making money was my passion, and I traveled by plane or car to make that money.

Even though male dealers would rob me, I still did it. I did not care much about going to school and spending years in school to obtain a degree to get paid. Especially when I could make it right away.

It felt great to tell the truth without feeling ashamed, and I hope it helped them. They were very patient with me, and they thanked me when I finished. I left fully ready for the next school.

I went back to the countryside and planned to go to my community school, an all-age school. I did some research to find the school's telephone number. I called and tried to speak to the principal of the school. Though I did not get the principal, I contacted the secretary of the school, who told me the principal was not available to talk to me.

I asked her if I could leave a message for the principal, but she asked how she could help me. I told her I would like to visit the school and talk to the students. I asked her to let the principal know I was available to visit her school with her permission, of course. I waited a few days and still had not received a return call from the school. I wondered if I was doing the right thing. Not to be deterred, I decided to go to the school in person. I put together a brief outline of topics to cover with the different age groups.

Early one morning, I went to school. When I arrived, I felt at home with so many memories of my childhood. When the security officer asked who I was, I replied, "I am a past student who would like to talk to the principal." He was nice enough to let me through the gate. It dawned on me that when I was a student at this school, there was no lock on the gates.

I skipped the office and asked to speak to the principal. I had to wait until she was free. When she came out to the waiting area, I jumped up from my seat, stretched out my hand, and said, "I am a past student, and I would like to give back to your students and school." She was so surprised! "I would love a few minutes to share with your students how much this school helped me to be a better person."

I told her I lived abroad, having left the island at age twelve. And I always desired to give back to my community, so I chose my favorite school on the island. She agreed to let me come back to talk to her students. I was overwhelmed by the opportunity to give back to my community.

I returned the following week and spent two hours talking with two classes. I spoke, and they asked questions. It was so amazing to truly give back by inspiring faith. It was an experience of a lifetime to be able to speak with the students. I got to express myself freely. I was willing to give more than to receive.

> Give and it shall be given unto you; good measure, pressed down, and shaken together, and running over, shall men give into your bosom. For with the same measure that ye mete withal it shall be measured to you again. (Luke 6:38)

Furthermore, I was grateful for this new opportunity to open and share my experiences in public. It gave me the courage and confidence I needed to get ready for the next one.

11

BE STILL

Humility was needed for me to be at peace with myself. Endurance and long-suffering were second nature to me because obstacles and disappointment were all I experienced growing up. But I learned to overcome all doubt, fear, anger, and worries of impossibilities. I learned to practice self-discipline, self-control, and patience. These tools helped me to gain more courage. I was always willing to go the extra mile, to just do it and keep going. But where was I going?

I had seven weeks left on the island and wanted to learn about this beautiful land that everyone talked about so much. I thought about where to go. Should I go to the beaches or visit my family? My mind was not ready to be still and relax, but my heart was at peace.

A Wandering Mind Is Hard to Keep Still

I chose to be alone until I could control my thoughts and tongue. I started to redirect my thinking about the outer things and focus on the mercy and grace of my faithful Creator. I sat and read my Bible all through the day and night. I saw verses that said over and over that he is the God of all comfort. And if I gave my life to him, he would teach me how to be still. I recalled an elderly friend who passed away from cancer. He kept telling me to keep the Sabbath, but I did not understand what he was talking about when he said to, keep the Sabbath a spiritual journey."

I spent a lot of time researching the meaning of the Sabbath and how to keep it. I knew most of my family members only attended church on Sunday. Only Jews kept the Sabbath, and though not a Jew from birth, I loved Yah. The Sabbath Days were something different for me.

I desired to discover my purpose on earth. I found chapters and verses in the Bible that said the heavenly Father knew me from my mother's womb and was the author and finisher of my faith. His words jumped out at me. They touched my heart and brought tears to my eyes. It left me wondering if he knew me from before the foundation of the earth. I needed to find out what he wanted for my life. And after weeks of researching, studying the Bible, and listening to church services on the radio and the song "Becoming Still," I was learning to trust in him.

I was running low on food, so I went to the city to do some shopping. I did my shopping and headed back to the bus stop, where all the transportation was parked and marked according to where one needed to go. As I walked, I wondered where I could find a Sabbath service to attend in this city.

Near the bus stop I heard someone say, "My people, you need to study the Bible for yourself and keep the Sabbath day holy."

I looked to see who said it. I listened to him and noticed that he was handing out papers, but no one was taking them. I immediately went over to him and said, "I will take one of those papers." I then asked, "How can I get in touch with you?"

On the bus ride back to the countryside, I read the paper. I was grateful and humble because the paper was filled with Bible verses. It was divided into sections on how to study the Bible. The information was just what I was looking for all this time. I knew God helped me that day. The day I met Elder Ricketts began my journey of deep scripture searching, studying, and keeping the Sabbath day holy. I kept smiling with joy and thanked God for his help.

I learned more from the Bible because of the paper I took from Elder Ricketts. It was a guideline, and I used it. I was so committed to learning all I could about the Highest. I gave all my time to studying the paper, and it increased my understanding and faith. I was now learning how to be obedient to the spirit within.

Two days passed, and I decided to call Elder Ricketts to find out about the Sabbath service. He told me it was on Saturdays at ten in the morning. He did not have a church but fellowshipped at his home with other brethren. He encouraged me to study the scripture and to call him if I had any questions. He was willing to help me, and I was so excited to know I finally had someone with whom I could share the Bible anytime.

I made sure to visit him the following Saturday. I met other sisters and brothers who were studying the scriptures. It was exactly what I longed to do with others. I had not fellowshipped before I met Elder Ricketts. He spoke to me about Christ, his life, and his resurrection. How he died for me and had risen. I did not understand what he was saying, but I was open to learning.

Elder Ricketts told me about Sabbath day fellowship and worship and how important it is to keep it holy. Sabbath was on Saturday, from sunrise to sunset. There could be no cooking, cleaning, or shopping. This was new to me. Since I was a child, I was always told that housework and shopping were done on Saturdays. *How can I do this?* I wondered. I thought of ways to change my mindset so I could do this. I humbled myself and became still. I had to learn how to plan my days to make sure I obeyed the Sabbath day. At first, I felt conflicted, overwhelmed, and nervous whenever I did any chores on Saturday. I had to remind myself to do all my shopping, cooking, and cleaning on Friday, and then sit and study the Bible all of Saturday.

I learn more on Saturdays than on any other day. I was feeling so much joy that I often called Elder Ricketts to share what I was experiencing by studying the Bible. Nothing was the same anymore, and I now wanted to share the Word with anyone I met. I went back to Sabbath services to learn how to fellowship with others. My time was—and continues to be—spent seeking to know the Creator of heaven and earth. I took the paper with Bible verses and handed it to anyone who dared to speak to me. I tell them, "I am here to do my father's work."

If people asked why I was alone, I told them, "I am about my father's business." All I wanted to do was share the new love, the good news I found in the Creator. I thought everyone had the same faith I did but soon realized I was wrong.

It rained a lot during January. The news reported harsh weather and recommended staying home if you did not have to travel. A few hours later, something strange happened. The skies were clear, and the weather was excessively hot and dry. Suddenly, the radio announced an earthquake warning. I thought I heard wrong. *An earthquake in Jamaica?* I went out to see if the report was accurate, but the weather looked great to me.

I walked back into the room because there were no signs of an earthquake. That was when I felt the shaking. It was something I had never experienced before. I went back outside. The trees were violently swaying, dancing back and forth. And the wind was whistling so loudly. The two-story building, I was staying in was shaking, moving as if it was ready to fall over. The wall surrounding the entire property started to stagger like a drunkard. My heart sank. I was so frightened, stunned to see and feel the earth shaking under my feet. I started to pray to God, "Please help me, and keep me safe from this earthquake." My heart melted within me, and the blood left my body. My life flashed in front of me.

There was one other person in the yard at the time. He said there had been an earthquake, but it stopped. He was so calm. Meanwhile, I was speechless. That was when I went to my room and got on my knees. I prayed and asked for protection and guidance. I thought of my children, my family abroad, and what would happen to them if something happened to me. Not only that, but I also worried about the uncertainty now that I was alone. Would they find me in this disaster? I vowed to give my life to God from that moment and to live by his will and according to his scripture.

> Who comforteth us in all our tribulation, that we may be able to comfort them which are in any trouble, by the comfort wherewith we ourselves are comforted of God. (2 Cor. 1:4)

Now the Bible made sense to me. It was so important for me to know his words. I saw the Creator's power in the blink of an eye. It was so sudden and swift, but now, it was as if it did not happen. I had seen his power and might for the first time in my life. I became completely still at that moment.

That afternoon, the news reported that at 2:10 p.m. on January 28, 2020, an earthquake of 7.7 Mw struck eighty-three miles north of Montego Bay, Jamaica. It was the biggest earthquake in Jamaica's history. The earthquake unit recorded a 5.4 magnitude earthquake on January 13, 1993. Back on June 20, 1692, the Port Royal earthquake caused devastation.

Now more than ever, I needed to know how to serve him because he is the way, the truth, and the life. The foundation of truth is in Christ. I committed myself to keep every Saturday as my Sabbath day, learning to worship and praise him. To be still in obedience and long-suffering.

My children called me that night. I was in tears while talking to them about my experience. My children said they heard the news and right away hoped that I was safe. My daughter was ready to come back to the island and stay with me until I was ready to go home. I agreed. I stayed committed and focused on studying the Bible and going to Sabbath services with Elder Ricketts and all the brothers and sisters in faith.

> I beseech you, therefore, brethren, by the mercies of God, that ye present your bodies a living sacrifice, holy, acceptable unto God, which is your reasonable service.

> And be not conformed to this world: but be ye transformed by the renewing of your mind, that ye may prove what is that good, and acceptable, and perfect, will of God. (Rom. 12:1–2)

> For whatsoever things were written aforetime were written for our learning, that we through patience and comfort of the scriptures might have hope. (Rom. 15:4)

The Bible tells us to bring our bodies, minds, and souls under subjection. This was the highlight of my vacation stillness—the seal of faith and truth.

12

COVER YOUR CROWN

I was enjoying my vacation spending my time knowing about the Almighty, Creator of all creation. At the end of February, my daughter and her baby came back to the island. The driver took me to the airport to pick them up. I was incredibly happy to see them again. I hugged and kissed the baby so much that she was happy. My family was with me. Not all of them, but I was pleased with their company. We planned how to use our days wisely.

The month of March was approaching fast. Her birthday was the tenth, and we were to return on the twenty-third. This was my daughter's first time on the Island on her birthday. She was so happy to be out of the winter weather and in a warm climate. We arranged a day trip to visit the beaches and rivers and spend some time just relaxing. I did not want to take the local taxi or bus, so I rented a car. We drove to the city for the day and bought all we needed for the baby. We picked up enough groceries to last at least two weeks.

I kept the car for a week, and we went on day trips using GPS to get around Jamaica. We had lots of fun driving from parish to parish. Some of the roads were good, but others were full of potholes. I was happy to have the experience of driving in my homeland. Our greatest adventure was Negril, the tourist hub in the west. It was a long drive; at one point, I thought we were never going to get there. But my passion to keep going helped me to find it.

Negril was new to us, and we did not know the best beaches to go to for a swim. I was so tired from the long drive that we chose to stop and take the baby for a swim and have some lunch. It was getting late, and I did not want to drive back in the night to where we were staying. We made plans to go next time with someone who knew the place well.

During the second week of March, I asked a family friend if he would accompany us to Negril, and he was willing to go with us for the day. We left early, picked him up, and headed to Negril. We arrived in three hours. He took us to the right spots. The white sand beaches were just like the pictures in vacation magazines. It was so beautiful I wanted to stay there on the beaches. This was an amazing time for me—especially since it took us four to five hours with the GPS to get to Negril the first time. We had a wonderful day. My daughter was happy to see it for herself. It was the best day trip so far. We left Negril before it was too late. After we dropped him off at his house, we headed to where we were staying.

I was now spending most of my time on weekdays with my family. On Saturday, I went to the city to attend the Sabbath service. My daughter and granddaughter would accompany me, but she did not understand my need to go for Sabbath.

And she noticed that I was very dedicated to learning how to become the child my Savior expected me to be.

After a while, I invited my daughter to join me for Bible study. She was open to learning, and it made me happy. I practiced with her to do a fellowship. We would read the Bible for an hour or two and talk about the Creator. I was still smoking and drinking a little. But after a while, I did not feel comfortable doing it and reading the Bible. I told her, "I believe that I should stop drinking and smoking." It surprised her, but she agreed that it made sense since I was learning more about God.

I was ready to be baptized. I made plans with Elder Ricketts to baptize me the Saturday before I had to return home. I had no doubts. I was ready.

My daughter wanted to have a gathering for her birthday, and I always tried to do my best to make her happy. We went to the supermarket and bought everything we needed for the party. I asked a family I knew from the river to come over and celebrate with us, and they agreed. The day before the birthday party, we were having fun just being in Jamaica, chilling and feeling proud of ourselves for driving around the island.

Suddenly, we got some unwelcome news from abroad. We looked at each other in disbelief. The news was worldwide, and we had to take it seriously and act immediately.

This was not a part of our plans for a big party on the weekend. And the following weekend, I was ready to be baptized. I called our family to find out if the news was true. My eldest son said it was. This was important. There was a pandemic, and we needed to come back now. I wondered what the pandemic had to do with the last few weeks of my long-deserved vacation on the island.

We listened to all the radio stations we could find. All reported the same thing. It was confirmed by our prime minister's request that those visiting from aboard cut their vacations short and return home as they were planning to close the port of entry.

Suddenly, all our plans changed. We had to call the travel agent to get an earlier ticket home. We canceled the party and brought food to family and anyone else in the area.

We prepared ourselves for the flight. It felt unreal. This world news changed my plans to be baptized on the island, in the ocean. I was looking forward to that day. Now I had to leave the same day that I was planning to be baptized and go back to the cold. I was sad and in disbelief because I was working on changing my life.

I prayed and kept humble and obedient to authority. I covered my crown with the Word of the mighty Creator because he always knows what is best for me.

I thank the driver for getting us to the airport on time. At the airport, we saw many people trying to get off the island before it was too late, and we joined them.

We arrived in Toronto safely. We went through customs and were cleared to go home. I was a little sad because I had to cut my vacation short and return to Canada because of the pandemic. Most flights were canceled. People were panicking over food and toilet paper shortages. The new world order meant most people worked from home. Everything possible was done online—school, shopping, and ordering fast food. I noticed that many major companies made huge profits, and the stock market was soaring. The rich were getting richer; the poor were getting poorer.

I did not get baptized. We were forced to stay at home and wear face masks until further notice. All this was new for everyone in our home, but not for me. I worked for years as a CSR technician in a hospital, sterilizing medical instruments. Working there, I had to wear PPE for years in a small space. I was one of the first people to complain about the heat and the environment we had to work in.

Our manager tried her best to help make our working conditions a bit easier.

The world was changing now, and we needed to adapt to what many called the new normal. I worked on myself, my children, my grandchildren, and friends so that we could get through this tough time. I prayed every day, especially on Saturdays. This would help us to stay focused on the Creator of heaven and earth.

I covered my crown with His Word and strengthened my spirit to get ready for whatever might come our way.

13

CANNABIS SHOPS

Mi spliff, mi friend. MJ is my friend.

Jah alone rules my head. I am willing to adopt his vibes. Just do not leave me day or night. Can you comfort me until the end?

MJ rules my meds. Oneness is in you, love is in you, and charity is in you.

It never asks when or why. And it does not refuse me when I cry. It comes wet, dry, or bent. It never talks back, only turns black after a long puff. Can I turn back?

When everyone left me, it was ready to roll up to me and keep me company. Lonesome feelings take up my mind when you are not around all the time.

But we must end; I just do not know when. I started when I was ten.

I used to hide to take a puff. That was the superb stuff, back then. They consider it illegal and underestimate your power.

They accuse you of all the wrongs in the world and offer it to our youth. Discriminate against you for so long, trying to hide the truth. What an evil plan.

I remember one summer in 2017. I was down and out for ganja. I almost lost my mind when my money was tied up, and I could not find a dime. I dreamed of you all day and night. When I did not have my ganja near me, it did not feel right.

I was incredibly surprised when my doctor asked me about natural herbs. I told him I used ganja sometimes instead of pills. The pills made me more ill. I felt like I was dead. I walked and talked slowly because of the pills. Not only that, but I also found out that I could get a license and get my ganja as a new medication to use along with the pills.

As a test run, I went online and purchased my meds. I bought Sativa and Indika. It felt good because in three days, the mail carrier delivered my ganja. This was a new thing that is now available in the market.

They fought against the Rastas as far back as 1940 to 1943. The first Rastafarian community was in Kingston, Jamaica, founded by L. P. Howell. The area was named Pinnacle, and they grew crops like yams and ganja. Ganja was considered illegal. The police would raid them often and arrest or sometimes kill anyone they found with ganja, or its new name, cannabis. The government took over the ganja and now call it the "healing plant" (Cannabis Healing). Still, the people are under pressure though it was supposed to lead to the healing of the nation.

Furthermore, you are the best-kept secret in Babylon. But for how long?

They break the commandment, "Thou shall not steal."

MJ, you rule the crown. Who can stop you now? Whatever is in the dark must come into the light.

I share my experience with all because it brought long-suffering and division to the people who did not know the truth. They did not want Rastas to profit or make a living. Propaganda made people think it was a vicious drug and that anyone who smoked it had a bad habit. But now, the world is okay with it. Where is the moral in this?

Rasta man who used the herb, and get a fight in earlier years, but now cannabis is on the stock market. Workshops are open and available to everybody to learn about their benefits. It adds to their monopoly, the money game to run the economy, but only 1 percent can afford it. They take the seeds and hide them. Who will compensate the ones who suffered and died because of them, the ones who died for a spliff?

But now ganja is legalized. It is the new trend. Cannabis is the best-selling and the quickest-selling plant on the planet. Everyone talks about it. Who will monitor the 1 percent who reap the benefit from ganja?

This is a rat race, and I see Babylon's footprint all over it. That is why I must quit.

Mi spliff, mi friend, you saved them again. The world's economic problems, you solved them. Now you are free to leave your country, travel overseas, or grow at home. People can do whatever they please. New world order, you can share it with your mama and papa. But give me the homegrown ganja; it is the only one that is better. Now, ganja is taking a flight, so the price is going to be sky-high.

Millions of pot shops are bringing the economy back. It is a one-stop shop; it is now easier to purchase all you desire. The crusher, the grabber, and the different-flavored paper to roll up the ganja.

You can go to your nearest drugstore, shopping malls, convenience stores, and shops. You can order online. It is now an A-class drug as a central services product. You are kicking down the doors, and you are in every store.

Four corners of the earth have adopted you. They open next to bakeries, banks, churches, and courthouses.

"What's that, mi a fi look back?"

Your style and design are blowing their minds. Pot shops in every area, one-stop ma-say. They wrap you up so properly, I must introduce you to my mama.

Fast-food joints have nothing on you now. All grades of ganja with different textures and colors. Candy, gummy bears, dark chocolates, and cakes for the munchies.

No need to hide. You are the new groom or bride for a ganja smoker.

I am shocked to see how many people line up at the pot shops for their fixes. More than at churches or doctors' offices.

One thing mi a fi say, "This new strain can never be like when I used to smoke with my papa. One pull from the vine and I come alive."

The promotion and advertisement placed on this product to the youths of this world are misleading and present an illusion, which is overwhelming. Pot of lies that I can talk about from my experience. I am waking up from this world of deception. I know now that every time I smoked it, I was giving my energy to a false god. He was running my head, but I have changed my moral compass.

No more ganja for me because I am healing naturally through faith from the Creator, who keeps my mind, soul, and body fit. He removes my desires for all worldly things. He cured me of Babylon illness.

The Holy Spirit within me helps me to overcome the blindness of pleasing the flesh with the spliff. The flesh craves the sensation of feeling high, relaxed, and conscious to make good choices. But it was a false hope.

Is It Healing the Nation?

I said I am healed without it. I live in the Spirit, so there is no need to feed the flesh with the spliff. I eat the Word and drink from the Holy Spirit. I am liberated from the spliff, so salvation and grace cover my face.

I am no longer under the deceiver's fire. I gave it up on January 14, 2021, because I found my Savior.

Get a grip and let go of the spliff. You can do it before you become stiff.

14

ARISE OUT OF YOUR SLEEP AND SLUMBER

Knowledge is now, it is what I require. For the
earth shall be filled with the knowledge of the
glory of YHVH, as the water covers the sea.
—Habakkuk 2:14

Wisdom continued to increase, so there was no need to retire. I
still hoped for a better tomorrow. When I arose from my sleep and
slumber, my desire was now to know my Creator. My hope was and
is to always be one with Him.

I had to find a formula and apply it because knowledge was the new
income, and I felt I must drown myself in him. So I had to increase
my knowledge. I did not have to look too far to see it because it was
deep inside me.

Simple Life, Quiet Flight with My Savior by My Side

Let us seek true wisdom and perfect beauty in his
holy law and holy gospel.

Give us the spiritual eyes, ears, and hearts to obey
your truths.

Our Creator knows our sitting down and standing.
My mind is set free when I remember thee.
You show me that all is possible once I trust in you.

This world is temporary and full of corruption and illusion. Through
lust, envy, greed, hatred, and so much more, we are distracted from
the knowledge of our Creator. Without truth in our lives, we become
like wandering lamps, lacking godly knowledge and wisdom. We
are living for the moment, unaware of the possibility of eternal life.
He alone controls today and tomorrow and the eternal past, present,
and future.

We are the veins of Christ.
We are God's vineyard.
Fruit of righteousness.
The light of this world is full of the knowledge of
truth.

The illusion of this world shines false light, making people lose their
value in life. The masses crave it now. Humanity's desire to belong
to someone or something is the secret of the world. The vanity fair
of this world offers the pleasure of sin for a season and the shadow
of the city of destruction.

All Is Designed to Distract You from Knowing Yourself

We must learn to overcome all the earthly things the world offers
us and realize we are all children of the Highest and be willing to
do his will. This is a massive deception and illusion for humanity.
Isolation is due to misunderstandings; it is one of the deceiver's

tricks. This was brought about not only by outer circumstances but by inner conditions.

The beginning of wisdom is to fear him, our heavenly Father. Living in the now changes my mind and heart toward life. I am aware and alive now by grace, mercy, and his forgiveness.

Without Christ, we become eternal wandering lamps. He is the light and lamb. He is the way, the truth, and the life. God gives us eyes to see, but some of us use them to look for things in the world. But what if we were blind? What would we use? Our ears. (Though five senses are not enough for me because I know six senses must be used.) That is why he gives us ears to hear if we cannot see. Unlike the animals, he made us in his image and likeness to be able to see and hear him. Some people are more interested in seeing or hearing the things of the world than the truth.

I was one of those living for the things of the world. I learned how to seek him and to put him first in everything I do. I learned to pray to Him to keep me focused on doing his will and steadfast in his righteousness, and not to be distracted by the illusion of this fallen world (Matt. 11:20–30).

The older I have gotten, the more I long for youthful days. My energy and strength were fading because of all the disappointments in my life. I became a wandering lamp. Because I did not cultivate my life around doing the right things, I had to pay the price for not seeking him first for knowledge. I was drowning in the things of this world, living according to what I was seeing and learning. But his grace and mercy found me.

After I learned about my Savior, I started to follow his law of love, which is Christ Jesus. The path of wisdom is paved with long-suffering, faithfulness, uprightness, righteousness, and truth. Learn how to abide with him, and he will abide with you (1 John 3:23–24).

"Those who fear, (reverence) God, believe and obey Him with trembling in faith will he give them wisdom. For the Word of the Lord is right, and all his works are done in truth" (Ps. 33:4). He will renew us as an eagle through his love for us and make us youthful again. Do not waste your youthful days in vain glory.

> So teach us to number our days, that we may apply
> our hearts unto wisdom. (Ps. 90:12)

As wandering lamps, we must seek salvation. But who gives us salvation? Only one man can give us salvation. He's the Holy One of Israel, Emmanuel, the life-giver. His way is my journey to everlasting peace within. His direction and purpose for my life were missing from the beginning.

Our work shows us if we are living righteously or unrighteously. How we treat others reflects on us whether we are godly or ungodly. Judgment day is when we must answer Abba Father.

> If any man among you seem to be religious, and
> bridleth not his tongue, but deceiveth his own
> heart, this man's religion is vain. (James 1:26)

> Let nothing be done through strife or vainglory; but
> in lowliness of mind let each esteem other better
> than themselves. (Phil. 2:3)

> But avoid foolish questions, and genealogies, and
> contentions, and strivings about the law; for they
> are unprofitable and vain. (Titus 3:9)

Take hold of yourself and give back to the Creator. That is our expected duty. Let us hear the conclusion of the whole matter: Fear God and keep his commandments for this is the whole duty of man (Eccles. 12:13).

Do not waste your time on the negative things that do not benefit you. These include anxiety, worry, anger, sadness, stress, doubt, disappointment, and resentment.

Pay principal attention to his holy presence in your life. He deserves all the praise and worship. He is the Master of creation. Keep seeking for truth, and truth will find you.

"They grope in the dark without light." (Job 12:24–25).

I was seeking the right way to live. I was getting so much runaround from humankind until I discovered my Savior and the King of saints.

And Jesus said, unto them I am the bread of life, he that cometh to me shall never hunger, and he that believeth on me shall never thirst" (John 6:35).

I am no longer hungry or thirsty for the things of this world. My wandering days are over because I know the owner of the breath of life. We can aim to live lives that are upright, honest, honorable, and just so that the next generations will see and learn from us the knowledge of fearing our Creator.

> By humility and the fear of the LORD are riches,
> and honour, and life. (Prov. 22:4)

Our sinful and corrupted bodies will not last forever. But the knowledge we impart to others will. We can subject our bodies to fasting and pray to the only living Master to help us overcome the massive temptations of the flesh.

Temptation is just an invitation to sin. The flesh does not confess, only the spirit.

> And as it is appointed unto men once to die, but after this the judgement. (Heb. 9:27)

> Heaven or hell is a choice; we will enter by our will.

I am renewed in my mind in the knowledge of him. I am steadfast that learning about the Creator and his words will save me and help me to overcome the enemy of my soul.

The Old and New Testaments were veils that were opened for our learning.

15

SOULISH GENERATION

This soulish generation finds it difficult to let go of worldly things.
We live by what we can see, hear, and touch, not what is unseen.
We are lost until we find the secret of self.
When we find ourselves, we find joy and inner peace within.

Glory is within the spirit of the knowing.
Glory freely arises from the truth.

The only way we can truly please him is by becoming sincerely obedient and living according to his rules. We cannot think that just reading scriptures, singing, and praising him will cleanse and qualify us to be righteous. He is looking for us to do the right things in our lives and not whatever we please. Following his way and will is the only way. Self-control and self-discipline are needed to help us develop the right mindset to give honor and glory to the King. Our soulish lifestyles will never bring glory to him. Pride and selfishness only bring separation to everyone inside and outside the churches.

Sociability and perception gives us false hopes and dreams that are acceptable to this world's lifestyle, which makes us feel comfortable in the forbidden, sinful, evil, and illusionary world. Its goal is to change the mighty, the powerful, and the purity of the Creator's children. The Prince of the power of the air goal is to change the Word to the world. Only one letter will lie to you and destroy humanity.

Where are our morals today? Where are the true prophets of this age?

This generation is impatient. Both young and old work are to be recognized in this fallen world.

> O generation of vipers, how can ye, being evil, speak good things?
> for out of the abundance of the heart the mouth speaketh. (Matt. 12:34)

> Ye serpents, ye generation of vipers, how can ye escape the damnation of hell. Soulish people's mindset is those who live in the mind and seek attention, gratification, and happiness. They are never satisfied even with themselves. (Matt. 23:33)

Someone suffering from soulish behavior is experiencing a disconnection from the inner spirit. The individual is unaware of his or her identity and chooses to be like others. These are the people who complain about what they do not have or what someone else has that they want. They often criticize everything and everyone. It is easier to embrace unrealistic behaviors and lifestyles when they see other people's joy and assume that their lives are more difficult than those of others.

They are unaware of their negative criticisms and indulge in vain and unprofitable conversations with their evil tongues. Soulish people are double-minded. They live to please the world and corrupt the Word. Perception and prejudice are the strongholds of their minds. They tend to blind most people to the realities of life.

> These are they who separate themselves, sensual, having no spirit. (Jude 1:19)

They look up to the Joneses or any other name they can achieve to gain status. This has nothing to do with spirituality. They live only for now, not for the everlasting. Their perception is sensual, not the true spirit. Furthermore, they do not see the need to get to know or give themselves faithfully to the One who created them. Nor do they understand that this body is a temple. And it belongs to God.

> For what is a man profited, if he gains the whole world, and loses his own soul? (Matt. 16:26)

What Should Someone Give in Exchange for His or Her Soul?

Soulish people suffer from a lack of faith. They speak from their emotions and feelings in their minds, which tells us what is in their hearts. If the heart is not cultivated toward God and his righteousness and truth, we seek only what feels good to us. We often seek someone to love and nurture our emotions and feelings, always seeking approval from others and not putting our confidence in him.

Some people deny the existence of the true and living King. Some honor him with their lips but not their hearts.

> Howbeit in vain do they worship me, teaching for doctrines the commandments of men. (Mark 7:7)

16

THE TWIXT, WE GOT FIXED

He is so merciful, compassionate, and patient toward his chosen people to have faith in him.

> Have we, not all one father? Hath not one God created us? Why do we deal treacherously every man against his brother, by profaning the covenant of our fathers? (Mal. 2:10)

Our faith is placed in all that this world is offering us, our governments, politicians, doctors, our cars, and our home security systems. And that is only because we can see them. This is a twixt that causes the illusion of the mind.

Real faith is unseen yet believed. When we trust in the infinite Savior, he will help us. He is faithful, and his promises are sure; he cannot lie. Nothing is what it seems. Always remember to read between the lines and the spaces between the letters.

It is now 2021, the end of the year, and there are more natural disasters and sickness, lawlessness, and two deadly diseases. There is no love in people anymore. Everyone is so impatient, and that's a wrong attitude. They call it COVID-19, Omicron, and more variants. And there's monkeypox. The government and health officials promote, publish information about, and push the masking mandate along with a vaccine with double or triple booster shots to help stop the spread. But is it working? More people with it are dying than living, giving people false hope.

It was all human-made, everything.

They are still celebrating the holidays, killing babies, and worshipping forbidden idols. The plan is to change the entire world from good to bad. The new world order is their agenda, and pagan practices and mass events will be changed for that reason. People are forced to be locked down inside their homes while they plan and scheme their online programs to brainwash and instill fear of the future. Their next move is total control of peoples' minds. They forget him.

"If You Plant Bad Seeds, Don't Expect to Get Good Fruits"

When I study the Word of the Master, I find comfort in knowing that his words are true and faithful. He promises a hopeful future and an everlasting life. We are living in a dying world, and his grace is all that we need to sustain us.

> Therefore, I say unto you. Take no thought for your life, what ye shall eat, or what ye shall drink; nor yet for your body, what ye shall put on. Isn't life more than meat and the body than raiment? (Matt. 6:25)

I keep these passages from the Holy Bible in my mind. They leave me speechless because he is willing to provide for us in every way. But in this world, people are so caught up in their external feelings of needs and wants that it misleads the masses into spiritual and physical deaths.

The LORD Is My Shepherd, I Shall Not Want

Most faithful saints understand the tricks of the deceiver. But some still are caught up in his traps and illusions.

> But blessed are your eyes, for they see and your ears, for they hear. (Matt. 13:16)

I am grateful for my Savior in my life because I was lost, but now I am found. It is a love that I cannot explain. It is so powerful in my heart. I do not feel alone. I am complete with him and confident about myself. I look forward to knowing about him.

I am learning how to use my ears to hear and my eyes to see the changes in myself and others. I have a heart of compassion, kindness, and patience toward humanity. I am learning to overcome the old man and stay focused on Christ's characteristics within myself.

> Therefore if any man be in Christ, he is a new creature: old things are passed away; behold, all things are become new. (2 Cor. 5:17)

> Another parable he put forth unto them, saying, the kingdom of heaven is likened unto a man which sowed good seed in his field. (Matt. 13:24)

> For there shall arise false Christs, and false prophets, and shall shew great signs and wonders; insomuch that, if were possible, they shall deceive the very elect. (Matt. 24:24)

We are living in the end times of prophecies, line upon line and precepts upon precepts. The entire world is set on fire with more pastors, preachers, evangelists, spiritual healers, palm readers, witches, and others quoting the Bible, sharing their beliefs, and reaching others still caught up in the evils of this world. How can we escape from ourselves or save ourselves? Only his infinite mercy and the grace of his forgiveness will save us. He can do more in our lives than we can imagine or desire.

No Man Can Do What He Can Do for You in Your Life

> Therefore if any man be in Christ, he is a
> new creature; old things are passed away;
> behold, all things are become new.
> —2 Corinthians 5:17

Faith is the inner fire that will keep burning when you feed on the Word of God. Once we follow his laws and statutes, our faith in Christ will open the inner spirit that we need to get closer to Christ.

> For we walk by faith, not by sight. (2 Cor. 5:7)

The Holy Spirit is the fire in our lives. We can connect to the inner flame when we are obedient and prophesying, giving our beliefs about the end times and what we need to do to be saved. It is so overwhelming with the wisdom of the Bible's words and the preaching and teaching about our King. The world is full of so much information but little knowledge and understanding about the true and living King. The Holy Spirit is the leader and teacher of humankind.

For the earth shall be filled with the knowledge of the glory of the Lord, as the waters cover the sea. (Hab. 2:14)

Forasmuch as ye are manifestly declared to be the epistle of Christ ministered by us, written not with ink, but with the Spirit of the living God; not in tables of stone, but in fleshy tables of the heart. (2 Cor. 3:3)

Who also hath made us able ministers of the New Testament; not of the letter, but of the spirit; for the letter killeth, but the spirit giveth life. (2 Cor. 3:6)

It is what the Word makes of you, not what you make of yourselves. He will build your life upon his rock. I built my church based on the truths said to the ones who obey him. We should be open and willing to help one another. That is one of the Master's commandments: "Love one another."

We must talk to him often in prayer, songs, and praise. Just remember he is always watching and listening to his children. He answers our prayers for sure.

We can build a close relationship with Him. There is no one more trustworthy and faithful than our Savior. When you give your life to godliness, He will help you in every way.

Faith in the Word of Yahweh, or Faith in This World?

Having faith is the only way to get your everlasting flame blazing. Faith never looks at circumstances. Unbelievers do. When we truly surrender ourselves and live, walk, and talk righteously, we will never live in lack.

> We are having the same spirit of faith, according as it is written, I believed, and therefore have I spoken; we also believe, and therefore speak. (2 Cor. 4:13)

Faith is a habit and an invisible strength within; it is the Holy Spirit. It is stronger than our mental and physical strengths that help to direct our lives. Put no faith in the flesh. That is the only way. Faith in the flesh is false living. With faith, we can please the highest, and with him all is possible.

My Evidence Is God's Word, and Faith Is the Answer

Our eyes are not only made for us to see the things of this world. They are also meant to look for faithful things of the Spirit. The nine fruits of the Spirit all carry a seed.

> But the fruit of the spirit is love, joy, peace, long-suffering, gentleness, goodness, faith, meekness, temperance: against such, there is no law. (Gal. 5:22–23)

> So then they which be of faith are blessed with faithful Abraham. (Gal. 3:9)

How do you sow seeds in this world?

Can your seed be duplicated so others can learn from it?

How do you live in peace, uprightness, faithfulness, and joy?

Faith is letting go and letting God.

17

INSIDE THE COMPASS

Peace within comes from our hearts. It is an act of compassion, openness, and willingness to share only what it has within. Love is a seed of faith without becoming intimate. Love is kind, patient, and faithful. "Greater love hath no man than this; that a man lay down his life for his friend" (John 15:13).

Love worketh not ill to his neighbor. Therefore, love is the fulfilling of the law.

Uprightness is a great habit. Humility and kindness are the true ways to get everlasting love to grow. What makes individuals different in this world is what they have inside and how they share it. There are people of righteousness and unrighteousness, godly and ungodly characters.

The Holy Spirit Can Only Live by the Spirit and Truth in Faith

The flesh is dead when we walk in the Spirit. And when you walk in the Spirit of godliness, we walk with him. I thank the Holy Spirit for his guidance and protection.

The Word of the King is the only tool that makes the flesh submit to the Holy Spirit. His Word can heal us, cleanse us, and save us from all our sins. Thy Word is a lamp unto my feet and a light unto my path. In him I found life.

> What know ye not that your body is the temple of the Holy Spirit which is in you, which ye have of God, and ye are not your own? (1 Cor. 6:19)

His Word Is Powerful

This is the generation of vipers who are so impatient in every way and everything they are doing. They lack humility and are unwilling to wait for his direction in their lives. Just learning to work hard and be good is too much for them. They want it now. They want to be successful now, get rich now, and want fun now. Not only do they lack humility, but they also lack respect for others. But they line up at the bank to get their money, food, vaccines, booster shots, and other things. I have noticed that they have patience for are the things of this world. But are they willing to line up and wash their sins away?

When a person goes to church, it does not make them a Christian. When you become obedient and faithful to the Word of truth, is when the Holy Spirit resides within. He will lead and teach us the things of the Master. There is no godliness in having one foot in the church and the other in the world. Living in the Spirit, one becomes Christ-centered.

> Watch and pray, that ye enter not into temptation: the spirit indeed is willing, but the flesh is weak. (Matt. 26:41)

Watch ye and pray, lest ye enter into temptation.
(Mark 14:38)

Ignorance Is Not an Excuse; It Is Dishonest

Our Master is the original Creator of heaven and earth, and everything is his. There is no price on the Master's love, but a man loved darkness rather than light. There is no price on hope and faith, but if we abide in him, he will abide in us. His love has proven that there is no price on righteousness. But there is a great reward if we obey the commandments and moral laws.

The Wages of Sin Are Death; the Gift of God Is Eternal Life

The definition of wages is a fixed regular payment, typically paid daily or weekly, made by an employer to an employee, especially to a manual or skilled worker.

The word "wage" is an action word. This means whatever we do, whether in action or deeds, we must give an account for it.

There is a day of judgment. We read in Jeremiah 25:14, "For many nations and great kings shall serve of themselves of them and I will recompense them according to their deeds, and according to the works of their own hands."

I live with faith in my heart. There is greater power than what I can see. My King has used me in so many ways to help those who are struggling with faith. All the challenges and obstacles that I had endured and learned to overcome never changed the love I have for my Creator and others. It only made me stronger.

My faith is like a seed that is planted in good soil. I become grateful and humble toward others. I apply lots of patience and care, knowing my faith—my seed—will grow once I show genuine love. The willingness to hold on to his promises is his thorough faithfulness. My faith hath made me whole and strong. I thirst no more.

I cannot see him, but I know he is with me and in me in every way and every day. Faith is more precious than gold. My Savior is alive, and he listens to me when I pray to Him.

> But without faith, it is impossible to please him: for he that cometh to God must believe that he is and that he is a rewarder of them that diligently seek him. (Heb. 11:6)

Avoid dilution of any kind. It is an illusion that can hinder your faith.

Do Not Look at Your Circumstances; They Will Defeat You or Grow Larger

Trust in Him. Keep your heart fixed on the King, and he will give you your heart's desire if you remain faithful and true.

His fountain of faith is for all of us. We must have faith in our hearts for spirit of truth manifest in our life. Trust in Him, and he will be there for you.

Our compasses are set for faithfulness and truth, no matter what it encounters. Our compasses have built-in lights that indicate our directions once we choose uprightness and are obedient to his will and way for our lives.

For whom he did foreknow, he also did predestinate to be conformed to the image of his son, that he might be the firstborn among many brethren. Moreover, whom he did predestinate, them he also called: and whom he called, them he also justified; and whom he justified, them he also glorified. (Rom. 8:29–30)

Blessed be the god and Father of our Lord Jesus Christ, who hath blessed us with all spiritual blessings in heavenly places in Christ. According as he hath chosen us in him before the foundation of the world, that we should be holy and without blame before him in love. Having predestined us unto the adoption of children by Jesus Christ to himself, according to the good pleasure of his will, to the praise of the glory of his grace, wherein he hath made us accepted in the beloved. (Eph. 1:3–6)

Elect according to the foreknowledge of God the Father, through sanctification of the Spirit, unto obedience and sprinkling of the blood of Jesus Christ: Grace unto you, and peace, be multiplied. (1 Peter 1:2)

We can strive for masteries in this world, but it is considered self-mastery. Some will achieve it. Some people strive to be successful in sports, academics, and other things that will give them the honor and fame this world has to offer. But there is another knowledge that only a few will dare to endure to achieve. One must live in obedience to the will of truth only and become a servant of the Highest.

Know ye not that they which run in a race run all, but one receiveth the prize? So run, that ye may

obtain. And every man that striveth for the mastery
is temperate in all things. Now they do it to obtain
a corruptible crown, but we an incorruptible. (1
Cor. 9:24–25)

And if a man also strive for masteries, yet is he not
crowned, except he strives lawfully. (2 Tim. 2:5)

If a man, therefore, purges himself from these, he
shall be a vessel unto honour, sanctified, and meet
for the master's use and prepared unto every good
work.

Flee also youthful lusts, but follow righteousness,
faith, charity, peace with them that call on the Lord
out of a pure heart. (2 Tim. 2:21–22)

Having the truth will help us to strive toward perfection, no matter
what may occur in our lives. His grace and promise are true and
faithful until eternity. No one else can offer us this assurance.

The servant of the Lord will strive according to their faith in him
and his Word to save us from all unrighteousness and ungodliness.
One's inner compass can be cleansed and sanctified and justified by
living in obedience to the Creator.

We can live for truth and justice in this world but only if we believe
in Him who died and rose for us. "And Jesus looking upon them
saith, with men it is impossible, but not with God: for with God all
things are possible (Mark 10:27)

In meekness instructing those that oppose
themselves; if God peradventure will give them
repentance to the acknowledging of the truth. And

that they may recover themselves out of the snare of the devil, who are taken captive by him at his will. (2 Tim. 2:25–26)

We can change our inner compasses to suit our heavenly Father. Nothing is too hard for him if you are doing it for those who love him.

> And if children, then heirs: heirs of God, and joint heirs with Christ; if so be that we suffer with him, that we may be also glorified together. For I reckon that the suffering of this present time are not worthy to be compared with the glory which shall be revealed in us. (Rom. 8:18)

I cultivate my inside compass with the Word of the King. He is the author and finisher of my faith. I choose to be obedient to his will and his way. I am an ambassador for my King, Yeshua, our Messiah.

18

WHEELS OF POINTLESS ENDEAVORS BRING MANY SORROWS

Sorrow is a sword in the wrong hands and used incorrectly. It can seduce the spirit and the mind of the inner man. Unkind words can leave the heart and soul shredded like paper. Strings of cruel words spark one to be angry.

I Had to Learn How to Get Angry but Sin Not

> What is sorrow?
> Does sorrow come in a row?
> Does it come today or tomorrow?

Sorrow is like a wheel of endurance that sits in every corner of life.

> For godly sorrow worketh repentance to salvation not to be repented of but the sorrow of the world worketh death. (2 Cor. 7:10)

> Who stops to help an injured or dead animal on the roadside?

Who cares for that soul that does not get buried
in a hole?

Mr. Sorrow's duty is to rob all souls of their blessings and grace.
And then leave them in misery. His brand creeps all over the world,
looking for someone to stamp. Immoral thoughts put into action
are full of destructive behaviors with many deceptions, fears,
resentments, and much rebelliousness and anger.

A broken compass invites plenty of sorrow, misunderstandings, and
misleading feelings that weaken every spark. When we display a
false reality, like gold is precious and beauty is forever, out of all
our negative elements come selfish accomplishments. This behavior
triggers pride and vain imagination of things to come. "Mr. Sorrow."
Everything under the sun is vanity and vexation of the spirit.

We need to know how to operate our moral compasses to detach
ourselves from unhealthy behaviors, relationships, places, and
things. Remember: sorrow is like a spinning wheel. Examine its
reason because it comes like the season. We did not ask for it, but
we need to know how to deal with it.

19

THE UNFAITHFUL GROOM

His vow sounded sincere until he could not get his way.
Yesterday, she seemed full of joy, bliss, wisdom,
understanding, and patience.
The next day, she lost her temper so badly that she
did not realize her groom was unfaithful.
He took her for a run and left her feeling dumb.

What happened to that calm, loving, patient, and understanding girl from the day before? She lost it. The man she married lit her fire stick, and suddenly, she had an outburst over something she could not fix.

Sorrow Is a Wheel with Many Sparks

It overwhelmed her to the point she sat in a yoga pose for hours, feeling dumb, numb, and speechless. As though there was a knife in her heart over a pointless task. She could not breathe because her emotions got the best of her and left her mind in a frenzy. Confusion engulfed her soul. She was caught in a maze of many twists and turns. Mr. Sorrow and Sir Disappointment crept into her life. She tried to endure the emotions that rushed to her mind, heart, and soul. *Does it even matter?* She wondered. She saw herself as that lost girl with lots of pointless endeavors. She tried to look cool, but she felt like a fool.

She rose to talk but was unable to speak or walk. Only a smile came from her eyes because she was torn apart, trying to understand where she went wrong. But it came back and blinded her mind. She wanted to move but was unable to escape from his grip.

She was physically sick and mentally wiped by such an unfaithful man. All she could do was to keep cool and pray to Yah for humility and understanding of how to overcome this sudden blow. She learned to harness her energy when upset or challenged. Patiently embracing the good with the bad and then determining what was best for her sanity and to set herself free. It taught her how to self-talk. She learned how to reprogram the brain to receive what her heart desired by staying focused on the righteous task at hand. She has learned to let go of false, unprofitable feelings and emotions and to accept. She created a space within her mind with godly words and broke the thirst for more. Pointless endeavors were a wheel she learned to control and let nature take its course.

20

FAITHFUL ASSURANCE: ONLY HIS TRUST IS GUARANTEED

Faith and belief are not the same things. Just like a coin with different sides.

Faith is not a feeling or favor. Our faith comes by hearing and Word of God. Our Creator is—and will always be—mystical, unseen, and unsearchable. As is his infinite creation.

> And by him, all that believe are justified from all things, from which ye could not be justified by the law of Moses. (Acts 13:39)

One's faith should not stand in the wisdom of human beings but in the power of the living King. Therefore it is of faith; that it might be by grace. To the end, the promise might be sure to all the seed, not to that only which is of the law, but to that also which is of the faith of Abraham; who is the father of us all. (Rom. 4:16)

The life-giver is faithful and compassionate, in authority, and fully expressed at the beginning of creation. He is omnipotent with the power to do good or bad. "See, I have set before thee this day life and good, and death and evil (Deut. 30:15).

> It is in the power of my hand to do you hurt but the God of your father spake unto me yesternight, saying, take thou heed that thou speak not to Jacob either good or bad. (Gen. 31:29)

The more I lean unto my Savior, the more wisdom he gives me to know that he oversees my life. And Moses said unto the people, fear not for God is come to prove you and that his fear may be before your faces that ye sin not. (Exodus 20:20)

God spoke to Moses about the people who had evil in their hearts and were disobedient even to Moses. It is written in scripture that they shall not praise or worship any other gods. But the people hardened their hearts and did not listen to Moses. This misbehavior brought curses on them that have been passed from generation to generation. And the children wandered in the wilderness for forty years and bore whoredoms until their carcasses were wasted in the wilderness.

They spent forty years in the wilderness, but did we learn anything from that story?

Abraham was a faithful man and became the father of many nations, fulfilling one of God's promises to him. He was obedient to the Master and built an altar to show his reverence. He offered to sacrifice his only son, Isaac, at Jehovah-Jireh.

> Know therefore that the Lord thy God, he is God. The faithful God, which keepeth covenant and mercy with them that love him and keep his commandments to a thousand generations. (Deut. 7:9)

We must create a new us through our faith so that when we are united with God, we can bear good fruits. When we try to do things on our own, without putting God first, we will fail.

It is written that from the time of old, the prophets taught people the way. Moses was one of the prophets, and the people still did not listen. Our world is full of many preachers, teachers, and bishops. But are there any prophets from God for us to follow in the twenty-first century?

> The Lord thy God will raise up unto thee a Prophet from the midst of thee, of thy brethren, like unto me; unto him ye shall hearken; (Deut.18:15)

> But they and our fathers dealt proudly, and hardened their necks, and hearkened not to thy commandments. (Neh. 9:16)

They refused to obey and rebelled. We are unable to do the King any favors. Not by our works are we saved but by his grace, so all we can do is to believe and have faith. Faith is the spark that started our belief in the Creator, who is the Alpha and Omega, the beginning, and the end. He is the way, the truth, and the life. Faith comes from believing in the Word of God. That is the truth.

The secret of faith is having an understanding and listening heart to be able to hear his voice. Once you pray and ask, he is willing to give you wisdom and understanding. We are creatures in seeing is believing, but what is visible in the things of this world are not what they seem.

Do you realize that we are all living unto ourselves and forgetting the grace and faith that is offered to us so freely?

Unbelief brings condemnation and festers sinful lust. We can avoid it, but it is a form of unbelief. When we use these words; if and maybe; whenever we pray to him, we change the chances that he will respond. Unbelief is a badge of doubt.

We must become committed and sincere. We must be dedicated to the law and grace. Be careful to obey all that is written as guidelines for humanity. Forgiveness is the first key.

> For there is no faithfulness in their mouth; their inward part is very wickedness; their throat is an open sepulcher. They flatter with their tongue. (Ps.5:9)

There is a great saying: "You see a man's face, but you never see his heart."

We can learn how to build our faith. We can walk in his light and not the darkness of illusion. Walk in faith and live. Avoid ungodly deeds.

When we live to please people and the world, we live to please ourselves. We walk in darkness. We will be like sheep led to the slaughter. Some people tend to walk on their ears or walk carefree until they have fallen into a trance or ditch, yet their eyes are open. "Where is boasting then? It is excluded. By what law of works Nay: but by the law of faith" (Rom. 3:27).

"Now; the just shall live by faith: but if any man draws back, my soul shall have no pleasure in him" (Heb. 10:38). But we are not of them who draw back unto perdition. But of them that believe to the saving of the soul. Faith is unseen by natural human beings. We believe and live in faith until death. It is a faithful saying that if we are dead with him, we shall also live with him.

Help; Lord; for the godly man ceaseth; for the faithful fail from among the children of men. (Ps. 12:1)

When a faithful and committed person fails, it becomes a lesson or a sign for all believers in truth to examine their faith. We can reevaluate where, why, and what caused our faith to fail. Living a perfect upright life is the hardest thing for humanity to grasp. We are programmed to think that we oversee ourselves. When we are unsure about our purposes, we are driven to follow and worship those who are successful and look to them as being approved by our society. When disappointments and failures, trials and testing come our way. We can learn to accept the good with the bad.

The world's people put their trust in the things they can see. The banks, doctors, the cars. They are willing to take a plane because they have faith in the pilot to fly that plane. But they do not put that kind of trust in the mighty Creator. Most of us also put our faith, hope, and trust in the pastors, evangelists, bishop-priests, and preachers with mega-churches. Not to mention crooked governments.

I have not hid thy righteousness within my heart;
I have declared thy faithfulness and thy salvation.
I have not concealed thy loving-kindness or thy
truth from the great congregation. (Ps. 40:10)

A sincere and God-fearing person operates from a pure heart. Any seed of hope and faith he or she planted, nurtured, and cultivated will grow into righteousness. When we plant a seed of faith in the earth, we set a standard for righteousness. With faith, one grows in dedication to the mark of a higher calling. I can put off the old man and be ready to do only the will of the Highest, which is my godly duty. The Good Book says, "For many are called, but few are chosen."

Many Christians are living only by what they can see and touch. Their faith is in seeing, and believing is exceedingly difficult for some to commit to faithfully. Everything outside us must be dead to the world because it is an earthly tabernacle.

Walking in the spirit and not in the flesh is extremely hard for some people to do. With a deeper awareness of the need to let him direct our paths, we will see differences in our lives. Once we take the intuitive approach to sanctify ourselves and set ourselves apart from these worldly deeds, our faith is increased.

"I will sing of the mercies of the Lord forever: with my mouth will I make known thy faithfulness to all generations" (Ps. 89:1). I will show forth thy loving-kindness in the morning and thy faithfulness every night.

> Night and day praying exceedingly that we might see your face, and might perfect that which is lacking in your faith? (1 Thess. 3:10)

Our lives will show us whatever we do while we live. Can a mother know what her child is going to be like before it is born? Our children only do what we do, not what we say.

> There is no price on faith; it is free.
> There is no price on hope; it is free.
> There is no price in his love; it is free, only believe.
>
> There is no price on grace or mercy; it is free.
> There is no price on the breath of life until COVID-19; it is free.
> No price on salvation. It is free because he already paid the redemption price for humanity. We owe him.

There is no price for the Holy Spirit that is within;
it is free only to seek him.
But there is a time for redemption; due.
Time for repentance; is now.
And the time to change; it is today, not in the
future, right now.
Our King and Master is so compassionate and ready
to receive us.

We must put Him first, not as an afterthought. We are never guaranteed tomorrow. But if we put hope, faith, and trust in his hands, he is faithful to raise us the next day. Death is welcoming to some people who are living with godly wisdom. But if we do not know where our souls are going, death brings fear.

All his commandments are faithful and true. They are our rods of correction and guide to righteous living. Without his grace, mercy, and faith, we cannot be saved.

> Time has no pause, and things are changing. But great is our Lord, and of great power: his understanding is infinite. (Ps. 147:5)

> This shall be written for the generation to come, and the people which shall be created shall praise the Lord. (Ps. 102:18)

Scripture teaches us to seek Him first, but we do the opposite, and seek Him last.

Are we here unto ourselves? Then why do we so foolishly put the things of the world before our mighty Creator until we are in some sort of trouble or at our wit's end or sometimes near death? Then we call on him: "Why me? Why now?"

Ignorance Is Not an Excuse; it is Dishonesty

When we refuse to give him respect, we become lost. Some of us tend to worship halfway, worshiping the creature more than the Creator. Our living Savior, who died and was resurrected for us, is alive and ready to help us through his grace and salvation. He is the Creator of heaven and earth. Who is more powerful? The God, the Lord, told us he created the heavens and stretched them out. He spread forth the earth and what came out of it; he breathed to the people upon it and spirit to those who walk therein. The secret is faith, obedience and hearing His voice. So, then faith cometh by hearing and hearing the word of God (Rom. 10:17).

> Now the just shall live by faith; but if any man draws back, my soul shall have no pleasure in him. (Heb. 10:38)

We can learn how to please Him.

We must know his will and be obedient to do his will.

21

WHAT IS THE TRUTH?

It is a question I often hear from many people, especially on social media. Many well-educated scholars speak about it, but none can readily identify, prove, or point out the truth. This puzzle is still unsolved.

When I was growing up, my teachers seemed to talk about the truth during lessons. Or were they only regurgitating what they had learned in colleges and universities? Now, as an adult, everywhere I look I can see people willing to tell their stories or speak their truths.

But what is the truth? How do you know something is the truth? To get a better understanding of the answers to those questions, I chose to listen more and talk less. I had to learn how to listen with my heart. I listen to a person speak his or her truth or tell a story, but I then check the words they use. A story sometimes can be partly true according to who is telling it.

Take, for example, a professor with several years of experience at a well-renowned college or university speaking to a bunch of students about the meaning of life. Will the professor speak from individual experiences or textbook explanations? Can the professor fully convey the truth of the origin of life without referring to the Creator of all?

Truth is a narrow path; few can find the entrance
to it.

This world is created for all to live according to one's ability. Once we are capable human beings; willing and open to give and take without malice or envy, we can find some peace with others.

We Can Live the Life We Love or Love the Life We Live: It Is Our Choice

To find security in this fallen world, one must be open to seeking the truth about this life. No one can tell you the truth about your inner self; you must seek it for yourself. As children, our parents will say, "Don't cross the street until you look both ways." We tend to listen because they were telling us the truth. But when we get older and can get married, we choose anyone we want, even if our parents tell us, "I don't think that is a good idea." We go ahead and get married and raise a family. When the marriage does not last, we wonder how they knew. Did our parents know the beginning before the end what was true? The result was that our parents or guardians knew what was best in part because when we are in love, love is blind.

The truth is within all of us. Yet only a few of us listen to it or are even aware of it. You may not grow up with loving and caring parents, but there is always someone who will expose you to the truth. But if you are not aware of his direction and guidance, you will miss it.

The truth hurts and can be extremely hard to accept.

We live in a time when wrong can seem right and right can seem wrong. How can we get through this madness without telling lies? Is this a test of our sanity or our souls? Every day we are forced to prove whether we are living in our truths or just living for the moment. Can we, would we lay down our lives for a friend?

My perceptions about life held me back because I was never good enough and that I needed to be successful for my family and friends to accept me. It was so wrong of me to want to be the best in everything so everyone would know my name.

The truth will show within us. We must work on ourselves to cultivate our senses—not just the five senses most of us were taught about, but the six senses our Creator gave us. Exercise your senses to know the good from evil and how to avoid immortal lifestyles.

Having godly wisdom and understanding increases our knowledge and helps us to fully comprehend how important godly knowledge and common sense are to survival. It is like a companion or a friend who is with you all the time, directing, guiding, and teaching you in every area of your life. This is the Holy Spirit.

The Holy Spirit has a never-ending relationship with God and is committed to humanity, especially with those who believe in the heavenly Father and His Son. The Holy Spirit is truly faithful until we die. Can we be faithful to an unseen truth? I am learning to live and walk in my truth, but I came to realize that most people are offended by the truth. I feel a sense of inner peace when I speak the truth, and the truth will set us free.

> Behold, I will bring it health and cure, and I will
> cure them, and will reveal unto them the abundance
> of peace and truth. (Jer. 33:6)

How did I come to my truth? I searched outside myself for years to try to understand life. Instead, I discovered my purpose in this life. I found nothing good outside myself, only trouble, disappointment, and deceptive and evil ways among people with agendas trying to control me.

It took me on a trip to my homeland. I wanted to be alone and be still. I wanted to learn what my inner spirit had been trying to teach me for years, but I had been too busy doing everything except getting to know my inner spirit.

I found out that I was never alone. That is true. I realized that my thoughts were not always mine, and the Savior was waiting for me to open and invite him into my life. He will guide me once I become mentally aware of his presence in my life and embrace him.

I learned three aspects of truth that are set in place for humanity to live in this world:

1. God
2. Word
3. Spirit

> Yah, (Jesus) said unto him, I am the way, the truth, and the life: no man cometh unto the Father (Abba Father), but by me. John 14:6

God is the Creator of heaven and earth. The Bible confirmed that he is the father of Abraham, Isaiah, and Jacob. The greatest promise of his Son, the Messiah, was fulfilled. He is the only true and living King. As were his birth, life, and crucifixion. The mystery surrounding his resurrection is unsearchable. He brought light and salvation to humanity and the world. He is our High Priest, who is faithful and merciful to everyone, especially toward his faithful saints who believe and obey his Torah and Law. He gives us grace and hopes to cultivate a personal relationship with Him.

The Word is the light of this world. It has power and might. One must live by his truth or die by the worldly mindset. It is your choice. The words we use can save us; they can also be our swords. So, we must be careful about what we say to others.

> For the word of God is quick and powerful, and sharper than any two-edged sword, piercing even to the dividing asunder of soul and spirit, and of the joints and marrow, and is a discerner of the thoughts and intents of the heart. (Heb. 4:12)

There are good and bad spirits. The Holy Spirit is good. The more we learn about the true and living God, the more his Holy Spirit will guide us. One must be grateful, committed, faithful, and obedient to the Spirit for guidance and protection that is offered to humanity.

> And the earth was without form, and void and darkness were upon the face of the deep. And the Spirit of God moved upon the face of the waters.

I read this verse over and over and prayed to Him to give me the wisdom and understanding of how to walk uprightly with integrity so I could know the truth about life. I kept seeking to know more about his way for my life and found verse after verse that pointed to him and his faithfulness and compassion toward humanity. No school, college, or university could have prepared me for this real-life transformation.

> The measure is not what you teach, it is what stays with the pupils.
> Remember nothing has been taught until something has been learned.

Sanctify them through thy truth thy word is truth.
(John 17:17)

I learned to discern if the person speaking is living according to the Spirit and the Word. Scriptures reveal the truth the fruit of the Spirit can never hide; see Galatians 5:22–23.

Furthermore, I was lost in the Bible, but I am now using it to guide me daily. The more I read, the more I want. I found out that I was adopted by Yah and an heir to his kingdom. And his grace, mercy, and salvation are for all who seek him. I studied his promises for me and learned that he promised to send the spirit of truth, who would guide me to all truths. With Yah, all things are possible. He and his promises are available to all who believe and have faith.

> For it is written for all to read and know, but God hath chosen the foolish things of the world to confound the wise, and God hath chosen the weak things of the world to confound the things which are mighty. (1 Cor.1:27)

At first, I did not understand the power that comes with reading his Word. It fills me with joy. I can be comfortable with just learning about him and his will. His way of life is what I desired.

The Spirit Is Truth

> This is he that came by water and blood, even Jesus Christ; not by water only, but by water and blood. And it is the Spirit that beareth witness, because the Spirit is truth. 1 John 5:6

God is the Spirit, the water of the Word, and the bloodshed on the cross. He is one. When we use the water of the Word and the blood in our testimonies, the Spirit bears witness. The floor of the heavens then drops out, and his presence comes to earth. The Holy Spirit lives in our temples, whether they are clean or unclean.

Regarding the law and the testimony, if they speak not according to his Word, it is because there is no light in them. The church is espoused, some faithful and others unfaithful.

The greatest controversy is between the truth from our Creator and the world's truth. Truth is for all who are willing and able to ask, seek, and knock; he will answer them. Anyone who refuses to believe is not willing to grow through long-suffering. If they cannot deny themselves worldly things, they cannot come into his truth, which I believe is forgiveness and acceptance—not perception or prejudice.

He gives us all we need to come into the knowledge of his presence in our lives. His Holy Bible is full of scriptures about how to serve him, which he gave to his chosen prophets to give to us. He said his people died because they lacked knowledge, and because they—we—are not seeking him with our whole hearts.

Many Are Called, Few Are Chosen

The truth cannot be hidden for long. Pride is deceptive. It is like a necklace that chokes every well-learned and wise person who claims they love Christ.

Any prophet who is not willing to be judged should not prophesy. Be aware of false hope. It is a slippery slope that will take us away from our Messiah's truth. Do not get caught up in people's ways or ideas. Many people seek ways to achieve life success outside of the

Prince of Truth. Some may come speaking in tongues, healing, and performing miracles. But they could be working with a different spirit that is not true. Mixing spirits is not good (Mark 7).

Do not accept Satan's destiny for your lives. Magicians, fortune tellers, astrologists, and false leaders with personal ambitions are among those who are not of Yah. Any rebellious spirit is witchcraft and not accepted in the house of the Holy One of Israel.

We must exercise godly discernment of the spirits we encounter daily. Are they walking in the truth or deception? Live for truth and righteousness, and the Holy Spirit, we lead you. The Spirit cannot lie. Do not worship only for worldly things. Worship to grow godly love for one another and to become the light on the hilltop that cannot hide. The church is espoused to churches, some faithful and others unfaithful.

The Kings of Kings is the truth, the way, and the life. The grand rail in the scripture to hold on to form eternal life. Keep it simple. We should cultivate the love of the truth, so we do not perish. Seek out the truth in the Old and New Testaments by studying the Holy Bible. Never go outside the scriptures.

Giving all the glory and honor to Yah. But the LORD is the true God, he is the living God, and everlasting king: at his wrath the earth shall tremble, and the nations shall not be able to abide his indignation. Jeremiah 10:10

22

PEACE OF MIND

Peace must come from within before we can get peace or peace of mind. Peace within comes only from the Prince of Peace, Yeshua.

> For unto you as a child is born, unto us a son is given; and the government shall be upon his shoulder: and his name shall be called Wonderful, Counsellor, The Mighty King, The everlasting Father, the Prince of Peace. (Isa. 9:6)

The World Peace Summit is held in various parts of the world. All heads of faith come together to find solutions for world peace. Though they talk about peace a lot, what kind of peace are they talking about?

> For my brother and companions' sake, I will now say, Peace be with thee. (Ps. 122:8)

How can they implement peace all over the world, in communities, countries, and cities? To get peace, we must first keep him in our minds. No matter how many or what laws are legislated, peace will not come to a person who does not know the Prince of Peace.

Peace does not carry poverty, crime, anger, sadness, worry, or resentment.

Evil is an enemy within.

Poverty is formed from the mind. World peace is an illusion.

There are only a few good men, and he who keeps his mouth keepeth his life.

Inner peace comes in a package full of compassion, godliness, patience, kindness, and forgiveness with temperance in every way to grasp the understanding of life. This godly wisdom can help many to elevate their thinking that will, in turn, change their behaviors toward life and others. Only inner peace can transform us out of lack. It is a long and lonely walk away from illusion, but it is the way to inner peace.

When an individual is lacking peace within or without, it is like a fig tree that is impeached and cursed by Jah. They become like branches that fight among themselves.

Peace is the inner energy of righteousness with an abundance of humility in love that will heal and bless anyone who finds it. First, peace.

The greatest sermon ever was the Sermon on the Mount by the Prince of Peace. It teaches us that all we need is salvation, and salvation comes only from him. We must watch our actions and purify our thoughts—most of all, our words.

As little children, we are taught to look out for danger. One of the most important things is never to talk to strangers. Yet the Bible tells us to beware of how we entertain strangers because we might be entertained by angels.

If the family does not have Yah in their hearts, then the home will not find peace.

Wrong behaviors come with consequences. But as we grow older, we move away from the principles of morality.

Discernment really should replace immoralities. Whether or not we know it, it is wrong to kill another human being. The killing comes in different forms in words or actions.

We can practice being the best athletes, win all the games, and get individual or team honors. But why is it so hard for us to practice and become perfect in our morality?

The world's masses are being controlled by a deceitful system that is programming them to be, feel, think, and act immorally.

Truth Is Out, and Deception Is the New Trend

The "prince of the air" created the greatest illusion, and its key players are the millennial generation who live in the web of destruction. This is the generation of disobedience, who are taken by the world network that take-away-knowledge, "godly knowledge" (Eph. 2).

The internet can be used for good or bad. You have heard that our eyes are the windows to our souls, but we need to guide them. The internet is designed to seduce the inner spirit and soul, capture the minds of humanity, and program individuals in the ways they want them to be.

The Holy Bible is no longer shared in the morning gathering at most schools.

This generation thinks life is easier, and it is OK to do everything or whatever they want on the internet. The internet promotes a life of secrecy. Personal interaction is out, and technical interaction is more acceptable for the youth. The way this generation socializes is so different than what it was twenty years ago. Outdoor playing with friends is not prompted as often as before.

Young people will sit in their boxes with a headset for hours, not interacting with others around them. I believe mental and physical depression will increase. How can we find true inner peace when everything is upside down, promotes false perceptions, and in pieces?

We must be strong to say no to immortality and yes to morality.

> Be willing to stand up for truth and righteousness.
>
> Be of good courage, and he will strengthen our hearts.
>
> Be kind, and you will find kindness.
>
> Live peaceably with everyone, and you will find peace.

We can strive to be people of godly morals and righteous choices. We will become the elective ones if we work on ourselves. We can only give what we have inside. So, examine what is inside you and clean up yourselves so you can help others to stand in the end time.

Inner peace comes when we learn to love our neighbors as ourselves. We cannot hide our inner thoughts and feelings from the Master of creation. One can only find peace in death unless one experiences the grace of God in great measure.

> Peace I leave with you, my peace I give unto you: not as the world giveth, give I unto you. Let not your heart be troubled, neither let it be afraid. (John 14:27)

Our blessing comes from our heavenly Father and His Son. When we believe, our living Creator hears us when we call on him. Be obedient; stand faithful to him. No one is more faithful, true, and able and willing to give us the inner peace we need in our lives.

Be a servant of the King, and his will and way can guide you.

> If my people, which are called by my name, shall humble themselves, and pray, and seek my face, and turn from their wicked ways; then will I hear from heaven, and will forgive their sin, and will heal their land. (2 Chron. 7:14)

> Come unto me, all ye that labour and are heavy laden, and I will give you rest. (Matt.11:28)

Only if one reaches a high spiritual level will he or she become patient and humble. They will then distance themselves from the things of the world as little as possible.

23

SLAVE TO SIN

The word "slave" and the act of slavery are two unpleasant words to swallow or understand. The conditions of being enslaved, in bondage, restriction, and confinement are considered long-suffering and hard labor. Slavery comes in so many forms from back in the fifteenth to the eighteenth centuries.

Human beings are used as human cargo for various purposes, including scientific testing, slavery, sex trafficking, and as mentioned, hard labor. However, in the twentieth and now twenty-first centuries, not much has changed. Humans are now more accessible through various platforms and black markets. Social media is one of the main sources of human trafficking for whatever purpose. Even though slavery was abolished in some parts of the world in the eighteenth century (in the nineteenth century in the United States), slaves and slavery are still alive.

When we get to know who our mighty Savior is and believe that he died for our sins and rose for our redemption, it will change how we think about each other. We cannot save ourselves from the wrath that is coming to humankind, but we can trust and obey his words for life. It started at the beginning, with the creation of Adam and Eve and in the days of Moses. Slavery was cruel and heartless back in the early centuries when everyone was enslaved for one reason or another.

Slavery was a tool used to oppress the poor and people in need. The underlying issues—evilness and greed—caused the vicious brutalization of humanity. African kings sold their people to slave masters. Slavery instilled fear in the people, who suffered in every way, including lack of food, education, and medical care. Women and girls lived in fear of being kidnapped or raped or both. Men and boys feared being killed or forced into armies for war.

Now, in the twenty-first century, social media is the new soul of slavery. This new device is imprisoning humanity's minds and souls. The masses invest their time and energy in the "soul tube" and feed their feelings and emotions on the World Wide Web.

The real issue is people living sinful, lustful, and criminal lifestyles on the Net. Now they can hide behind a computer and deceive others, trade children, and steal people's money. They can buy and sell everything, including pornography, which is the crown of the economic system.

The soul tube is the new norm. They are very trendy and widely accessible. There are libraries, cafés, and many other places where one can use the internet. Crime is in the palms of our hands. Using computers is not forbidden or illegal. It is easily accessible even to underage children. Everyone who reads or writes has an email address and can easily get connected. It is among the tools available to the enemy of our souls to capture the souls of the King's chosen people.

The prince of the air makes it easy for us to lose our ways. The internet is the wide and broad road leading away from the truth to destruction.

> Enter ye in at the strait gate; for wide the gate, and broad is the way, that leadeth to destruction, and many there be which go in there at. Because strait is the gate, and narrow is the way, which leadeth unto life, and few there be that find it. (Matt.7:13–14)

The narrow road is the right way.

> Where in time past ye walked according to the course of this world. According To the prince of the power of the air, the spirit that now worketh in the children of disobedience. (Eph.2:2)

This is the new way of living in the twenty-first century and even a hundred years into the future. Our eyes are wide shut. We are addicted to computers and phones, the new forces connecting us to entertainment, socialization, yoga lessons, church services, idol worship, online classes, and doing business all in the comfort of our homes. Working from home, not the office, is the new norm.

This Is the New World Order

Fewer humans interact face-to-face than in previous generations. There are increasing numbers of illusions online, making you think the person on the screen is like you. The natural way of interacting or showing affection to another is quietly eliminated over time. The internet is designed to be used for various tasks. It is up to the individual to do the right things. We allow violence into our homes in words and actions. Music, movies, and video games are fully displayed on TV and the internet. There is no sin in having a TV, computer, or smartphone. Or being on the internet. It is how we use it.

Over the years I have noticed an increase in Bible apps. They are trendier than physical Bibles. More people in the four corners of the world are finally being reached through this platform. Youths idolize role models they see on any platform. These include those who do not live with godly morals and integrity. And as we know, the soul that is lured into sin tends to be carried away from the truth and grace of our Savior.

If the son therefore shall make you free, ye shall be free indeed. John 8:36

All the hidden objects are in plain sight. It is so tricky. While you are reading from the online Bible app, pop-up ads appear to suggest, lure, and distract you to shop or join them. Such apps are the greatest misleading device that ever existed. It sets you up to fail in every way possible. There are symbols and signs that once we can read between the lines of the unseen and the hidden, you will find, "There's no secret in creation."

> Those who have eyes, let them see, and those who have ears, let them hear
> The secret of craving for momentary feelings that cannot be quenched.
> We are slaves to sin, and only his grace, mercy, and salvation can save us.
> When we are enslaved by the world and greed, we become slaves to the flesh and the will to serve something or someone, to feel fulfilled.

Obedient saints are not slaves to sin because they accept the cup of salvation. Christians are not free from the power of sin. There are Christians who live for righteousness, but some are blinded by sin and become its slave. Believers of the King of righteousness live in liberty and draw from the bank of heaven. And they never lose power once they are drawing from the right source. Knowing how much you are valued makes you walk in the likeness of his character. Being a Christian is standing on a solid rock while every other place is quicksand.

Christians must come through the fiery furnace of affliction to be refined. A true child of our Savior does not live to please people. Rather, the individual strives to serve the truth and help others. You can decree the principal character of a true believer of him.

Humility and sincerity are in faith and truth. Not every Christian is a true Christian as much evil is done in the name of the Holy One.

We cannot justify our sin.

> For many are called, but few are chosen. (Matthew 22:14)

> Not everyone that saith unto me, lord, lord, shall enter into the kingdom of heaven; but he that doeth the will of my Father which is in heaven. (Matthew 7:21)

> My little children, these things write I unto you, that ye sin not, and if any man sin, we have advocate with the Father, Jesus Christ the righteous:

> And he is the propitiation for our sins: and not for ours only, but also for the sins of the whole world. (1 John 2:1–2)

When we only put our hope and faith into the things of this world, we become tied up, distracted, disappointed, angry, worried, and fearful. It leaves no time for true fellowship or to have a relationship with him. That is what makes us enslaved to sin. The purpose of this life is to worship and praise our heavenly Father with all our minds, hearts, strength, and souls. He created us to praise and honor only him only; he is a jealous King. He told us to study so that we are approved unto him by studying the scriptures in the Holy Bible. Our hearts must be in accord with our Savior's will and ways. But some of us are so distracted that we become a slave to sin when we indulge in worldly affairs that consume most of our time and, therefore, forget to seek him first. Check if this is his will and way for our lives. Some people are ruled by the flesh, not the Spirit, yet we are spiritual beings.

To grow the fruit of the Spirit, we must first learn to accept the suffering.

> It is the spirit that quickeneth; the flesh profiteth nothing; the words that I speak unto you, they are spirit, and they are life. (John 6:63)

> For the word of God is quick and powerful, and sharper than any a two-edged sword, piercing even to the dividing asunder of the soul and spirit, and of the joints and marrow, and is a discerner of the thoughts and intents of the heart. We are slaves to sins when we walk in the darkness. Walking in the light we believe in Christ and obey his commandments and live. (Heb. 4:12)

> He that saith he is in the light, and hateth his brother, is in darkness even until now. (1 John 2:9)

> He that loveth his brother abideth in the light, and there is none occasion of stumbling in him. (1 John 2:10)

But he that hateth his brother is in darkness, and walketh in darkness, and knoweth not whither he goeth, because that darkness hath blinded his eyes. (1 John 2:11)

The world offers all the things to satisfy the flesh, not the spirit.
This is the example of a slave to sins, or slave to our flesh.
Then you can gain the whole world and lose your soul.
But they that will be rich fall into temptation and a snares, and into many foolish and hurtful lusts, which drown men in destruction and perdition. (1 Tim. 6:9)

Examine yourselves for the Word will make you or break you. The Spirit within will either change or remain the same. Then you will know the difference in your heart.

I examined myself and discovered I was so trapped in the pleasures of this world that I did not care about going to church or reading my Bible. I lived my life according to the world's views. I went to work and did whatever was needed to survive. I was more focused on becoming someone important to my family, friends, and business partners. I loved to work hard and play hard. I worked day and night for years without taking vacations or breaks. I was committed to working. I did not care about anything but getting paid. My best friends were my ganja, my money, and my four children. I was a slave to money and the things of the world.

My mind was set on success, building my wealth, and making my mark in this world. I wanted my family and friends to know I am successful and beautiful. I was enslaved to the idea that life must offer big houses, cars, clothes, and parties. I desired to share all I learned in this world and to leave a legacy for my children.

> Whose end is destruction, whose God is their belly, and whose glory is in their shame, who mind earthly things? (Phil. 3:19)

I was wrapped in sin, full of desire and pride to be the best and have the best. I gave my energy to things of the world, not knowing I was living in lust, adultery, and covetousness. I was unknowingly headed to hell. I was lost in the wilderness and living in darkness. I was blind and foolish until I found my heavenly Savior.

It took me ninety days of praying and fasting to become focused on His words. I was sold on, committed, and absolutely dedicated to serving my King in spirit and truth. That is what changed my inner being, and it will take the rest of my life to serve him.

Inner Illusion Is an Outer Pleasure That Pleases the Mind

There is pleasure in sin, but only for a moment. It is a brief comfort to the flesh. Our flesh lusts for all things, but the Spirit wants nothing. We cannot find truth in an illusion, and there are no lies in the truth. But we have an unction from the Holy One, who knows all things.

Slave to sin is a stronghold and bound with the things of this world that can never be overcome by any outer peace. A soul that is glued to worldly acceptance and approval of man is a soul lost in sin. The proud are far from knowledge of life and are choked by sin.

> Walk by faith, not by sight.

> Worldly possessions are temporary, but the inner
> spirit is forever.

The willpower to break free from the sins of the world is in one is will. It is a personal walk and dwells in heaven, not hell. Only through the Holy Spirit can we know him. The Holy Spirit is the power of our Savior.

> Love not the world, neither the things that are in
> the world. If any man loves the world, the love of
> the father is not in him. For all that is in the world,
> the lust of the flesh, the lust of the eyes, and the
> pride of life are not of the father, but of the world.
> (1 John 2:15–17)

Me can turn into we. Then the spirit of grace and mercy will manifest for humanity eternally. And the world passes away, and lust thereof. But he who performs the will of God lives forever.

Abide in him, and he abides in you. This is a promise from God.

When we invest in the things of this world more than we invest in his grace and mercy, we become slaves to this world. If we deny him, we become slaves to sin and live in perdition and darkness. We are never free.

Deliverance Is Not Freedom: We Must Be Born Again

We are quick to buy a ticket with the hope of winning the lottery. We hope to become successful and accomplished and forget who gives us breath and life and strengthens us with courage. We are quick to get married and raise a family and hope it will last forever.

Where to get a skilled professional and spend lots of time studying and making money. Nothing will last or manifest without his help.

We are so dedicated to being the best in the things of this world that we forget our Creator's laws and commandments. We are quick to give our love to things we can see, touch, taste, and smell and forget who gives us our senses.

> Our flesh delight in glory and honour and Our Creator will not share his with another. (Isa. 42:8)

We tend to worship the created more than the Creator. We cannot serve two masters.

> Mine hand also hath laid the foundation of the earth, and my right hand hath spanned the heavens when I called unto them, they stood up together. (Isa. 48:13)

He created heaven and the earth and nature. But people worship the sun, moon, nature, and diverse cultural expressions and images as their gods. Let us put aside the gods of ancient times, the ancestors who indulged in forbidden power and greed.

> The fool has said in his heart there is no god. (Ps. 14:1)

> For thou hast trusted in thy wickedness: thou hast said, none seeth me. Thy wisdom and thy knowledge, it hath perverted thee; and thou hast said in thine heart, I am and none else beside me. (Isa. 47:10)

There is only one eternal God, the Holy One of Israel.

He is the first and the last, the beginning and the end.

There are two powers in the world—the power of light and the power of darkness. I was raised in a rat-race society to hustle for material possessions and monetary gain. Then I learned to put my trust in Yah. The entire world strives to be or become something or someone other than itself. People are selling their energy to the lesser forces of this world and do not even realize it. People who are vulnerable, poor, and homeless are caught up in the snare of the devil's trap.

The desire to belong is based on lust, greed, and pride to satisfy the needs of the flesh.

> But godliness with contentment is great gain. (1 Tim. 6:6)

To achieve righteousness with Yah, we must become obedient only to his will and his way. There is no other way to everlasting peace within our souls.

> For as many as are led by the Spirit of Yah, they are sons of Yah. (Rom. 8:14)

The law is a set of rules that does not cover sins. So, offering and making sacrifices cannot and will not take away humankind's sins.

Grace cannot be earned, and we cannot work for it. We should not mix law and grace.

Can We Keep the Whole Law?

The law is designed to show us where sins lie in our lives. It is the King's way of diagnosing our good or bad deeds. The law dominates the flesh until you submit your life to truth. The law works on your fleshly nature, but we can put death to the flesh by having a personal relationship with the Holy One. He is not looking for a legal relationship. Rather, he seeks a spiritual relationship. By his Holy Spirit, we can write his laws on the tablets of our hearts. Then we must yield to the Holy Spirit that is within us. It is not by force but an effort to unify.

Sin Is an Assassin

We know that the law is spiritual, but I am carnal, sold under sin. The problem is within us, and nothing written or seen can change us until we change our hearts. If we are under grace, sin will have no dominion over us.

> To the law and the testimony: if they speak not according to this word, it is because there is no light in them. (Isa. 8:20)

Just a reminder of where we are coming from until now. All this was planned by humankind, not by him. They went ahead and reconstructed their plans for humanity hundreds of years before I was born. Universalism, globalization, and multidimensional processes were created for the world to attain some kind of oneness. The diverse cultures and economic and geopolitical conditions are under one umbrella, the technological world or one world order. This is called the global connection and global consciousness, but everything is at its peak. What else is left for us to discover? What is left to invent? Can a robot give birth? The human family is so unique and special in the eyes of the Creator.

The world is overrun with so much knowledge, and some people forget about the Creator of it all. The Heavenly Father forgives them for they know not what they have done.

24

MY MORAL COMPASS IS FIXED

Thy will be done, on earth as in heaven.

It is the macrocosm in the microcosm, overall.

In every tiny atom is the entire principle of creation. We are all creatures of the one divine Creator from the animal kingdom. Humanity links the soul, thymus gland, and our inner spirits of truth.

Hiccups are not popular, but everyone has them from time to time. Just hold your breath for a minute and experience the uniqueness. We all have the same experience.

Check your design and review all the old nursery rhymes. Do you still have that childlike mind? From beginning to end; as above, so below. Go to the root, and you will find the truth. There are gems in the rhymes like those found in humankind's life stories.

1. The three wise men and the star in Bethlehem
2. The gingerbread man
3. The three little pigs
4. The giant and the beanstalk

5. Popeye the sailor man
6. Red Riding Hood
7. Alice in Wonderland

As the Bible says, unless we become like children, we cannot enter the kingdom of heaven. The only way to be saved is to believe, accept him in your heart, be baptized, and walk in his light. Flesh circumcision cannot save us. We need to be circumcised by the heart, not by the body.

Heaven means our minds and the kingdom are within our bodies, and our bodies are the temples of the highest. Our thoughts are like brain waves of frequency and vibration of self. Godly and heavenly thoughts in our minds will heal the spirit and direct the heart to righteousness. Then the mind and body become blissful. I always keep in mind that this body is my vessel—vehicle—for this earthly realm. Some of us will find ourselves living in the minds of our feelings and emotions that rule the heart and the body. They can hide the inner man and the unknown self. Once we give our minds, hearts, and souls to his will and way, we become a superior individual who has chosen to walk in his light. And we are more compassionate with others. The inner person is hidden by many scars until we learn how to forgive ourselves and others.

What Comes Out of a Man Defiles a Man, Not What Goes In

> Howbeit there is not in every man that knowledge; for some with conscience of the idol unto this hour eat it as a thing offered unto an idol, and their conscience being weak is defiled.
> —1 Corinthians 8:7

Karma is drama, and the truth hurts.

We are created to be his children, his handmaidens, and as a royal priesthood for his coming kingdom. Our purpose in this universe is to worship and praise him, as well as to share and receive love.

Many people seek an experience without truth. Some Christians, guru masters, other religious people, yoga experts, and deep-meditation life coaches seek to be in touch with the mind, body, and spirit. All are hoping to line up the chakras for a better life, health, and prosperity. But the more we seek our ways, the more lost we become in human-made idolatry and vain things. We become bound in religious doctrines, traditions, ancestral cultures, and ideologies that cannot help us to connect to the full assurance of faith and truth.

Thou shalt have no other gods before me. (Exo. 20:3)

The only one who bears witness is the Holy Spirit. He bears witness because he is the truth. So, the Spirit, the water of the water, and the blood shed on the tree agree as one. When we use the water, it is the Word. When we use the blood in our testimonies and when the Spirit bears witness, the floor of the heavens drops out, and heaven comes to earth.

As a child, I was in many storms. The Holy Spirit was there for me even though I did not know of his presence in my life.

The truth is in the storm and how we react to the storm. The storm is testing one's strength or weakness for our Savior. His rain falls on the just and the unjust. The sun shines on the good and the bad. There is nothing above or below that he does not know.

When we come through a storm, we can then testify that our Savior saves us. All my storms transformed me to do better. A faith that cannot be tested cannot be trusted.

He was amid my storm when I was five years old and very adventurous. One day I climbed to the top of my parents' vehicle. I fell off and landed on a sharp stone in the center of my forehead. My family rushed me to the hospital, and I was out for days. I wore bandages over my eyes for months because the wound was right between my eyes. But family members said I was still a happy child during my recuperation.

By the time I was eleven or twelve years old, my mother who traveled at the time, sent me and my sister to live with her. I was not happy with the decision, so I rebelled. I did not take full advantage of the opportunity to go abroad and live in a new country. I felt unhappy, misunderstood, and overwhelmed. I ran away from home at age fourteen. I started to skip school and chose to be homeless. I was determined to return home.

I spent time with the children on the street, drinking and smoking. I started stealing to feed and clothe myself. This became a habit, and I started to steal more to make money. At that time, I thought, *I need to get my own place to live.* I was not sexually active because boys were controlling, bossy, and no good. I lived as if I knew what was ahead of me every day. I did not care to speak to any member of my family.

A family friend decided to find me and encourage me to return home or live with them. And I did. He had a family. They had a challenging relationship, and I did not like it because it was not like the freedom I had on the street. It was difficult for them to find work, and his girlfriend was often sick. It was very discouraging. We turned to the only sort of income I could provide. I hustled to buy food and pay bills. Now that I was adapting and perfecting my skills, I improved even more. Their friends sometimes came over for drinks and smokes, but I stayed in my room.

Over the years, I felt that I would rather be on the street than with them in their house. I had many chores and felt fully responsible for helping the family. But I eventually went back to my parents' apartment. That only lasted a few days, until my clothes were thrown out on the ground, and I left for good.

During this time, my dad lived in another country. He persuaded my mother to take my sister to help in taking care of me. I was happy to be around my family, but they were not pleased with my lifestyle. It was very new for them.

My sisters and I decided that we should put our money together and rent an apartment to share. I was happy because I knew how to hustle and would have a chance to go back to school once I had a place to live.

We rented a three-bedroom apartment, and I loved it. I had my own room, and our apartment was nice and clean. I remember we had a bathtub, not a shower.

Occasionally, we had a few friends there. I often went to parties and would drink and smoke ganja all day and night. My sisters and I dressed like triplets. We were the talk of the town, and I made lots of friends. Everyone thought I was friendly and kind. I loved to help in any way possible, and because of that characteristic, my name was popular on the streets. Not only on the streets but at dances and parties. I was a track star and dancer from an early age in my country and made some mystical moves on the dance floor.

My brother was happy to see us working together. I was back in school and doing very well. My math teacher, who loved all his students, encouraged me to study hard so I could do something great with my life. Most of my teachers said I had the potential to do very well if I only applied myself. I was willing, coachable, and well-mannered with everyone I met.

My sisters were so cool, and we got along very well. Other girls were jealous of us, but we did not care because we were bold, tough, and good fighters. We stood up to anyone. I was comfortable living with my two sisters.

One day while I was home alone—my sisters were out for the day—I heard a knock on the door. I was not expecting anyone, but a friend sometimes visited unexpectedly to get some smoke or just to say hi. I left my bedroom to answer the door. I looked through the peephole and saw a family friend. I was not sure what he wanted, but I opened the door and let him in. He asked for my family members. I told him they were out. He asked for my sisters. I was a little worried, but I politely answered that they were out too. I was not sure why he was at our house, but he said he came to me! I felt shocked and afraid. I froze in my steps and asked, "Me?"

He smiled. "Yes, you. I like you, and I want you to be my girlfriend."

I was lost for words. I did not care for this older, tall, strapped man. "Not me, please. I am not interested in any man. I am in school!" He grabbed me, pulling me close to him. He lifted me off the floor. I could feel my buttocks in his hands and his finger in my undisclosed area as he pulled me closer to him.

He was so strong. I tried to push him off, but his grip was hard around my little frame. I kept saying, "I am not interested," but he kept saying, "I want you to be my girlfriend." With such force he pulled me close to his face. His face covered mine, and he put his big, nasty tongue in my mouth. I could not scream or talk. I wiggled and pulled myself away and ran from him into my room. He ran after me. He held me down on the bed and forced his finger through my pants and into my private parts. It hurt because his hands were big. I jumped back, but he pulled me closer to him.

With one hand on my neck, he held me down. Then, on top of me, he forced his manhood inside me so hard it hurt. I tried to cry, but he kept forcing his tongue into my mouth. I kept fighting, but he was too strong for me to push off my body. He molested and sexually abused me. And when he finished, he whispered in my ear, "You are my girl, and now you belong to me. And if you tell anyone what happened, I will hurt you."

I was broken and terrified. I felt lost. My vagina and my legs hurt a lot. My sheet was very wet, and there was a cool liquid between my legs. I started to tremble. I was so nervous that I lay there curled in a ball and said nothing. And then he left. I waited to hear the door close before crawling out of bed. I hopped to the bathroom, sat in the tub, and cried.

My compass was broken.

I did not cry for help because I had trusted that he was a good friend of the family and I let him into the apartment. I opened the door and let him in. I was very naive. I never said a word to my sisters or brother about what happened to me that day.

Over the following months and years, he would suddenly show up at our apartment pretending to just visit. He would act as if I were someone he cared about. I hated to see him. I would leave the apartment and stay with my friends for hours, until I knew he had left. Whenever I went to a party, he would be at the party. He always tried to hold my hand, but I refused because I knew he was not a kind man. I am so grateful for the heavenly Father and his mercy to know the difference now. I prayed for forgiveness and mercy for that guy, and I overcame that moment in my teenage days thanks to him.

By the time I was eighteen years old, I was in another storm. I was shot in the face at close range. Then I got back up to speak to the person who shot me. I do not know why God saved me that day, but I thank him.

He was amid my storm when I indulged in the things of the world and left my two children, an eleven-year-old girl, and a seven-year-old boy. I took the weekend off from college and went on a vacation. It landed me in an island prison for two years for smuggling two kilos of cocaine. To get to this island, one must take two planes. First, an international flight and then a local twin-engine plane. I had no family or friends on the island, and during my time in prison, no visitors. The women's prison was on a rock near the ocean's edge. Thick, high walls surrounded it. The prison had been an old fort that was built in 1806. It was a place where the soldiers fought wars back in the early century. It was also used as a poor house, a leper colony, and a mental hospital. Now it was used to house fifty women prisoners, including me.

At first, this was so traumatizing for me. But I did the crime, so I must spend the time. The place was unfit for us to even be there, but we committed a crime and had to pay the price. My moral compass was broken again.

The prison area was blocked off from traffic, and no visitors were allowed. We were locked in a four-by-five-foot cell with four bunk beds and no restrooms. We were only allowed out of our cells for breakfast, lunch, dinner, and bathing time, about thirty minutes each time. We had to take a bath three times a day, an officer watching while we bathed. The bathrooms had no windows, and rain and heavy winds would come in whenever we were having a bath. The weather was up and down. It was often very windy and cold, especially when it rained.

The head matron was brutal. She ruled with an iron fist and did not care about our well-being. She let us stand against the wooden hallway as she looked us up and down. Then she screamed in our faces about our crimes just to remind us that we were not good enough for society. She made sure our time there was extremely hard.

I met one of the ladies who was in prison for life. She was locked in a small room with no windows. The woman was in solitary confinement because she was considered too dangerous to be around the other prisoners because of the horrible crime she had committed. There was no radio or television in the prison, so we could hear her beautiful voice when she sang. We could also hear her cry day and night. It was so sweet, but at the same time, it was very sad. She was crying out to him for forgiveness of her crime. Though the government told her she would never leave prison, her faith and belief in him for forgiveness kept her strong. She was a Christian woman.

It took me months to understand what had happened to her. It broke my heart, but I never judged her. Rather, I hoped I could talk to her someday. I would pass by her door and let her know that we were there for her. And I told her my name. We were not supposed to talk to her, but I did. I would sneak to talk to her and encourage her to stay strong. She had a hope that was beyond comprehension. He was going to let her out. Whenever she would cry and sing, the matron told her to shut up because she would die right there. But she had faith I knew nothing about. Her dream was for the Queen of England to visit the country and free her. That was her belief, and it happened.

The prison had tough rules, and I obeyed them until I got sick. I realized that we needed some sunshine, or I would die. The head matron hated the fact that I was not from that country, and I was not afraid of her screaming in my face. I would respond to her in a firm manner, which made her upset. As a result, she made my time more difficult in every way she could.

During my incarnation, I became ill and was transported to a hospital with chains on my hands and feet. I witnessed people dying around me, and it scared me to the point I planned to do something to make a difference, not just for myself, but also for the other prisoners. We spent most of our days and nights locked in our cells. I would read my Bible and meditate on how to tell the other inmates about my plans.

I was the only foreigner in that prison. I started to observe my surroundings and the on- and off-duty officers. I tried to figure out who was fair and caring enough to help me with my plans. My time in prison was hard, and I cried nonstop for two months because I missed my children and other family members. The ladies there were genuinely nice to me and encouraged me to be strong for my children. They understood that I had no family on the island, so they adopted me as a family member in prison. That is when I realized I need to toughen up and help them too.

My mother found out about the incarceration and ended up in the hospital. That broke my heart even more. What hurt me the most was the news of my grandmother's death while I was in incarcerated. I started to cry again because all I planned was to hustle and get big money to go back to my country to buy or build a house for my father and grandma. My heart's desire was to take my family out of poverty to a better life.

I wanted out of prison, so I started to rebel against the head matron. I would talk back to her and be locked in my cell for days. But I did not care. I wanted to hurt her so badly because she always reminded us that we were dirty to society. I made several jokes about her face and shape. I got into big trouble with the head of the prison and was labeled the troublemaker of the prison.

I had no contact with my children and family. It was ridiculously hard to think about how they were coping with my big sister. She was not nice, more selfish than nice. Everything was getting me upset to the point I thought about escaping, but I had no idea how or where I would escape to. The first four months were very hard on me. Every week there was a new female prisoner. Their crimes were more wicked than mine, and I tried not to think of mine anymore. I would talk myself to sleep saying, "I did the crime, I must spend the time," over and over.

My mother sent me boxes full of things for me to use while I was in prison. I shared them with all the inmates. I gave the matron a few things, and she became my friend. Her ways toward me started to change, and I was allowed to join them for Bible lessons. But sometimes she took things from us—like sanitary pads and body wash—and locked them away. Once I got my stuff taken away for not listening to her. I never understood why.

I knew how to braid hair very well, with or without a comb. I spent my time braiding the ladies' hair in the cell. One morning the head matron came in and asked, "Who is braiding and making all these big hairstyles here?" Everyone was happy and felt great about themselves. But I got in trouble for being creative. Her favorite saying was, "This is a prison, not a beauty salon. So, know your place." But after a while, I started to do her hair, and everyone loved it. She received many compliments on her hairstyle, and I became her hairstylist in prison.

She became more open and willing to let visitors come in. Before this time, only people who had family could visit. A group of ladies from a church visited. They were willing to sit and pray with us. But I wanted no part of it. I would sit there quietly until ordered to take part. I resisted for a bit. Over time I obeyed.

I started to enjoy the meetings with the church ladies. I was often the first to ask them questions. We were never allowed to touch them or take gifts from them. We would sing, pray, and hope for a change in the prison. I asked the church ladies to convince the head matrons to let us do some baking as an activity. It took a while and some meetings with the head of the prison, but we eventually got permission. The ladies would come and teach us how to bake cakes, and it was fun.

I then had another idea to help make our time in prison less stressful and to avoid becoming depressed. Some of the ladies were already suffering from mental illness when they killed their children. But none were ever diagnosed or received treatment. I started to encourage them to think positively about themselves. Some of the ladies did not have the opportunity to attend or finish school. I would sit with them and do the basics of reading, writing, and the alphabet. There was so much sadness in the atmosphere. I thought we needed to go outside in the sun at least once a week. I tried to talk to the church ladies again, but the head matron refused to consider this idea. She said I was pushing it, and I must remember that this was a prison, not a place for all these things. I knew sitting in the sun would help, so I decided to find someone who loved and genuinely cared about the prisoners' well-being. I wrote a letter in secret and asked one of the workers to mail it to me, which she did. I knew the consequences that could come from writing the letter, but I wanted justice and righteousness to rain on us even though we were prisoners.

Furthermore, there was no way to run from the prison unless one chose to jump off the cliff and into the ocean. We would surely die. Every day I waited for the head matron to come into the prison and scream, "Who sent a letter to the embassy?" But there was nothing for a month or more. Then one day a call came in, and I heard a scream. It was from the head of the prison, telling the head matron to lock us down. Everyone wanted to know what was happening and why there was a lockdown. I kept quiet because I was sure it was because of me. There was a young lady from a different country in the prison with us who had not been fully sentenced yet. She would cry every day. I was not the only foreign prisoner on the island anymore.

We were no longer allowed to meet with the church ladies or even bake cakes. We could only come out to eat and bathe. Right away I knew something big was happening. I hoped and prayed that someone from the embassy would come to see the conditions they had placed on us.

A person from the embassy did arrive on the island. We got a visit from the head of the prison; he was the corporal for the male and female prisons. He warned us that we were his prisoners, and the person who wrote the letter would be charged. I was escorted to the head of the prison by two officers in the town. I met a woman from the embassy she questioned me in front of the heads of the prison. I told her what was happening to me and the other female prisoners. I expressed that we were treated like animals. I told her about the conditions of the place they kept us in and that we never got to see the sun. I pled for her to consider us and our living conditions. I asked if she could implement a rehabilitation program for us. I was not looking for an uncomplicated way out but for some humanitarian support from the embassy and the head of the prison. They did not allow the embassy representative to visit the female prisoners. She wanted to make sure that I was not being tortured in any way.

Two months later, the head matron started to loosen up and change. All female prisoners were given two hours of sunshine and daily exercise.

I spent two years in prison with no visits from family or friends. When I was released, they made me immediately leave their country. Their government red-flagged me from ever entering their island. They said if I entered their country again, they would catch me and jail me for life.

We Cannot Have a Testimony without a Test

He was there for me when I was in a car accident. That accident saved and changed my life. I had many challenges. I lost the job that I had for over fourteen years. I was unable to function properly. I could not sit up for long or walk upright; I leaned to the side. I could not stand by myself. Lifting, pushing, and pulling were difficult tasks. I experienced severe chronic pain in the back of my neck, lower back, and legs. For two years, it was challenging to sleep. The doctor said I had a minor injury, but it would take a while for me to recover. I suffered serious whiplash from the car accident.

This was the final straw for me. I felt that if I did not change my way of thinking and living, I might end up back in jail or dead. The hardest and the best chapter of this book was reliving my memories to put them on paper. I have worked more on myself the year since my accident in 2014 than at any other time.

I researched and read many inspirational books to grow my soul and spirit in the direction of becoming a champion and to create a mindset able to master my thoughts and behaviors. I learned to empty my mind.

In July 2016, I changed the way I lived. I started to meditate every Friday from 6 p.m. to Saturday noon. I worked on staying consistent and dedicated to doing my one-day fasting, and it helped to strengthen my mind and increase my knowledge. I became a vegan in 2003 and ate less processed food and rice. I added more fresh fruit and vegetables to my diet. I incorporated an exercise routine to build up my energy level. I loved it. I made some decisions to work on my health and strengthen my mind so my income would increase.

I met nine millionaires in the space of two years after changing my mindset. I felt so privileged to be in the same environment with some of the most prestigious leaders, champions, and entertainers. I was humbled and grateful, excited to see their humility. I eagerly asked questions, but most of all, I listened, took notes, recorded, and took pictures. I attended many seminars and workshops in the process of getting to know myself and what I needed for my life. That was the most important lesson I got from all the amazing leaders and champions I met. That was the best part of my discovery of how to develop the right mindset to win no matter what happens.

I was working to become an Investor, so I first invested in myself. I bought some books and borrowed some books from the library. I spent lots of time reading and taking notes. And then I practiced what I have learned with my children.

I am still working to improve myself and my income and build a legacy for my children. I stopped working for people and worked more on how to strengthen my mindset to win without outside interference.

I am now considered unemployable. I am grateful for all the wonderful people in my life for that brief period. I have learned something from all the wonderful people in my path.

I traveled to learn more about improving my consciousness and building wealth. Now I feel obligated to share what I know with like-minded individuals and to act in the right way because all things are possible. I am grateful for the opportunity and blessings they have given me.

My journey began with accepting that I did not know anything. What I learned during my school years did not prepare me for the life-changing things I was experiencing. I changed everything about myself and my life. I got out of an unhealthy relationship. I filed for divorce and got it done in one year. I made the choice to trust God for everything, and I promised never to look back.

I am a better person because I now know my heavenly Father. He delivered me from the pit of hell and keeps my soul alive. For days and months leading to years, I cried and repented, asking for forgiveness for the way I was living. I admitted that I was a dreadful sinner, doing whatever I liked without acknowledging my Savior's love for me.

I read the Bible and believed. I accepted him as the only one who could change my heart with his Word. His words convicted my soul, and the Word of God cleansed me from all unrighteousness and sinful lifestyles. He has allowed me to do better, renewed my mind and thoughts, and changed my life for his kingdom. I am grateful for his mercy and grace toward me. I recognized his presence in my life, and I humbled myself and learned to follow his will in my life. I pray and worship my Savior every chance I get. And I am happy, willing, and pleased to share the good news with everyone I meet. I am his hand-made, and I now know the value of my life.

I am working on myself to become a servant for my King, Yeshua.

I am not of this world, just in this world. I am willing to inspire others to search the scriptures for themselves until they find the Holy One of Israel. The Holy Spirit is the teacher, guide, and comforter for all. I am his servant. I will wait for the new heaven and the new earth. I live for his promise, his inheritance, and everlasting life.

I study the scriptures day and night. He is my boss, my employer, my redeemer, and my eternal Savior. I am grateful for the comforter he sent to comfort me.

I am newly converted and baptized. I was baptized in the lake in Pickering, Ontario, with my daughter, Nika Stephenson, and Donna Beanie, my sister in Christ who lives in Montreal. She was converted from the heart and asked to be baptized during her visit to my home in Toronto.

A week before the baptizing, I went and prayed to my Savior for warm weather as it was not yet summer. He granted me warm weather on May 13, 2022. It was the type of weather one would love on the day of baptizing. I knew the water would be cold, but he gave us warm weather that day. I proved that he answers prayers.

I chose to be baptized by a faithful man of God, Elder Ricketts. He is a servant of the highest, and I can see is faithful to the Word, so I chose him to help me with my baptism. Though he lives in Florida, he was willing to travel to Canada to baptize the three of us. He and his wife were so faithful. Elder Rickett's pilgrimage began thirty years ago, when he was seeking the truth. He identified himself as a servant of Yeshua, the Messiah.

However, he received a vision to go to the island to reach the lost sheep and share the truth using only the scriptures. He has never been a pastor, but he is a lover of the Word. His message is that people must study the scriptures for themselves because church leaders are misleading the people. There are many false prophets in this world. I now understand that the only leader is the Holy Spirit. He is pleading to the people to repent and give their lives to the Holy One of Israel, Yeshua.

I chose to walk according to the Spirit, not the flesh. I am nothing without Christ in my life. Were it not for him, I would continue to be a wandering lamp in the decaying world.

To paraphrase the first line of the following scripture. Thy word is a lamp unto my feet, and a light unto my path. Ps. 119:105

> Jesus saith unto him, I am the way, the truth, and the life; no man cometh unto the Father, but by me. (John 14:6)

He has broken down the middle wall. He is our High Priest, so nothing can stop us from reaching out to him.

> If my people, which are called by my name, shall humble themselves, and pray, and seek my face, and turn from their wicked ways; then will I hear from heaven, and will forgive their sin, and will heal their land. (2 Chron. 7:14)

My moral compass has changed to the point that I feel his presence in my heart and the evidence in my daily life. I no longer find myself as a wandering lamp. I do not guess what to do or where to go because he is holding my hands and leading me on the journey. I have chosen to be single and become still in His presence until I can understand when my Savior is talking to me. I genuinely want to live for his will and purpose in my life. I changed my moral compass to walk according to his ways. I have no desire for the things of this world anymore. I have learned how to be humble and to pray in every situation because I know that he cares for me, and he promises to never leave me or forsake me. He is working on me, making me a new person. I gave my heart to Him and now walk in the Spirit.

I gave up drinking, smoking, partying, and vain babbling. I am willing to sacrifice my time and energy to know his Word every day. I spend a lot of time studying the scriptures so I can apply my heart to wisdom. I chose to dress modestly and cover my hair all the time. I am grateful for his patience with me because I have come a long way. I am on my pilgrimage, and he has placed some faithful servants before me to assist me on my journey.

> I will greatly rejoice in the Yahweh, my soul shall be joyful in my Elohim; for he hath clothed me with the garment of salvation he hath covered me with the robe of righteousness, as a bridegroom decketh himself with ornaments, and as a bride adorneth herself with her jewels. (Isa. 61:10)

25

HOW TO OVERCOME THE SMEARS OF DEATH

The last enemy is death, and we can overcome its devices that are set for humanity. Once we come into the godly knowledge of the law of faith, we can overcome its sting.

There are steps we can take to help us stand up to death. First, we must understand its purpose, whether sudden death, unseen, or sickness to death. Death is not the end; it is just the beginning of everlasting life. Death is not just a word but a moment that will come to humanity. Once we are born, then we shall die. But who can tell us our departure dates? Like a vacation that is planned, everyone has a departure date and an arrival date. Even if one prepares for the final day, he or she still does not know one's date and time of death.

The power of life and death is in his hands. No scientist or doctor can change death once God calls you home. No talks or research can manipulate God's plans. I chose to learn what is required of me before my date arrived. I chose everlasting life with my King, the Father of Abraham, Isaiah, and Jacob, my ancestors. It does not matter our status or wealth, wise or foolish, young, or old; in this life, we must die. How we embrace the moment it arrives determines one's strength or weakness to go through it. Our moral obligation to love one another is more important to the Creator of all. Keep in mind all his children are precious in his sight. Whatever self-discipline and principles we live by will show if we are connected to righteousness and uprightness. Through His salvation, faith, and grace given only by him to humanity, can we change our moral compass.

> Keep thy heart with all diligence; for out of it are
> the issues of life. (Prov. 4:23)

Prayers are the only hope. They can help us overcome the sudden feelings and emotions that come from death. When one comes into the knowledge of the heavenly Father and his will and way for their lives, one will overcome the snares of this decaying world. When we die, we are set free from sin. Death will no longer have dominion over us because we are under grace. This means our Savior already conquered death and sin for us. No word can replace the feelings when we lose a loved one, but if that loved one understood that his departure date was to welcome him, then we should celebrate and not be sad.

The Thing Is, This World Is Temporary: We Have the Choice to Live or Die

Sins are equal to death, and his grace and mercy will help the ones who are obedient to his will to live uprightly and righteously. "Whosoever love is life will lose it; but whoever loses his life for His name sake will find it. For all have sinned, and come short of the glory of God" (Rom. 3:23–26).

This world is full of so much evil, can any good come out of it? We must become sold on righteousness and everlasting life. And anyone who is a friend of this world is an enemy of God. A spirit of worldliness is attached to the people of this world. We are flooded with many religious systems with plenty of false prophets, false love, doing things your way, and misleading teachers. There are many wolves wearing sheep's clothing in the churches. What is right has become wrong. Who is qualified to judge the natural understanding of moral principles and change the unrighteous way of living? This spirit of worldliness is designed to destroy the foundation of truth that is in God. Its agenda is to promote the illusion of love, which is counterfeit love, working on the minds of people to corrupt their thoughts into doing evil. Furthermore, if someone is not committed to studying the Bible for themselves, it is hard to develop a biblical principle and understanding to walk in faith.

Who can control their tongues? It is the most powerful part of our bodies. The poison of the asp is under our tongues. The Bible tells us that we are his children. This verse expresses it even better: "My little children, let us not love in word, neither in tongue but deed and truth" (1 John 3:18). We cannot profess that we love our Creator and live any way we want or desire the things of the world. If we are friends of this world, we are enemies of God. "Ye adulterers and adulteresses, know ye not that the friendship of the world is enmity with God? Whosoever therefore will be a friend of the world is the enemy of God" (James 4:4).

If we love, we do not lie, steal, or kill. We will never do anything that is unrighteous and know in our hearts if it is wrong or unjust to others. We are obedient to His will and way for our lives.

As a child, I watched my grandmother, who was so committed and dedicated to her church. It was a place of reverence and holiness. Now, in the twenty-first century, the respect and love for the churches are gone. Most of the churches are out of order. All kinds of immoral lifestyles and behaviors changed my views on the morals of the churches. Most pastors are afraid to stand against the unrighteous and ungodly behaviors displayed by the people in their assemblies. Until this year, I had never heard of people fighting in the churches, much less money being stolen from churches. That is what the churches have been reduced to now. The new trend is to attend church in style. People usually go to church when they feel lost in sin and want to change their lives.

It is different now with the new generation. The goal sometimes is getting as many likes as possible to your posts on social media pages to show that you are part of a church. Dressing modestly is out; dressing however you want is in. Churches are big businesses and the fastest way to make a profit without tax.

Religious knowledge produces pride, and pride is a necklace. Religion is not a sound doctrine. Where is the sincerity in obeying the laws and statutes of God? Self-gratification is the new norm for most religious people.

Where all are under sin, as it is written, there is none righteous. No, not one. Only our Savior can change our hearts to walk according to his will in the dying world. We all want to be free from the troubles and struggles of life, with no sadness, no pain, no deaths, but only the Holy One of Israel can make it happen.

> Therefore, if any man be in Christ, he is a new creature; old things have passed away; behold, all things become new. (2 Cor. 5:17)

When His kingdom comes, there will be a new heaven and new earth for the former things have passed away.

If we wish to be free from fear and death, we need to get a full understanding of death.

O death, where is thy sting? O grave where is thy victory? (1 Cor. 15:55)

The human mind is limited compared to our Savior. One day to us is a thousand days to him, and a thousand days to us is like a day to him. We need his infinite wisdom and knowledge to gain godly understanding to survive in this cruel world.

We must live by facts, not by our feelings. Feelings and emotions are temporary senses we can learn to control. The world taught us never to talk to strangers, but it is written in the Bible that we should not forget to entertain strangers because some may be angels.

To free ourselves from the fear of death and to renew our minds and hearts, we must surrender all to our Savior. We must first accept the fact that we need to change from the heart and work toward becoming the person he wants us to be. Second, accept him as your Savior. And third, become a student willing to commit the time necessary to learn how to be a servant for his kingdom.

Our brains are like computers, and our hearts are electrical panels. If our computers are not working well, we are not happy. But if we keep our houses in order, the better they function for us, just like our minds and hearts. A well-organized home with clean rooms helps us to work effectively. Houses with many rooms are like our minds and hearts, which have different compartments too. We must learn to declutter our minds. Whether a small or large house, it can be productive and harmonious with consistent care. The inner environment is just as important as the outer environment. What we use to furnish our houses should be just as important as what we put into our minds and hearts.

When we keep our minds free from resentment, guilt, ungodly thoughts, and actions, our hearts will work with joyfulness and willingness. I chose to give my mind and heart to know his will for my life, and the Holy Spirit will lead the way.

Keep the mind clean and learn to empty unnecessary things.

If our minds conform to this world, we will always want worldly things. The world impresses on our minds to stand up and fight for whatever we want in this life. But God said the battle is his, and all we need to do is pray.

Prayer is powerful.

This worldly system is designed with several images of false perfection. They glorified death, leaving people with the illusion that when they die, that is the end. This false impression says that death is something to be afraid of. The current perception is that one must be successful and wealthy before dying. There is nothing about saving your soul so that you can live an eternal life. The original intention was for humanity to be immortal, but sin entered the world, and the natural order that God intended was upset. Death is the king of terror, and the gift of immortality is for all.

> I cannot plaster my mind with the world's false perfection. Where there is corruption and massive deception comes sin, violence, crime, and war. This is the illusion that this world has offered in the four corners of the world.

Everything I gain in this world is now foolishness, except my children. I never sought my Savior first. I must be dead to sin and self to be able to walk with the Messiah.

I plaster my mind and heart with the Word of God. His law and commandments will keep my mind firm. I learned how to write them on the table of my heart. I will not sin against him. I am mindful of who oversees my destiny.

> Marvel not, my brethren, if the world hate you. (1 John 3:13)

> For the wages of sin is death, but the gift of God is eternal life in Christ Jesus our Lord. (Rom. 6:23)

> Brothers and sisters, we do not want you to be uninformed about those who sleep in death, so that you do not grieve like the rest of humanity, who have no hope.

> But I would not have you to be ignorant, brethren, concerning them which are asleep, that ye sorrow not, even as others which have no hope. (1 Thess. 4:13)

For if we believe that Yeshua died and rose again, even those who sleep in Yeshua will God bring with him.

> For the living know that they shall die; but the dead know not anything, neither have they any more a reward; for the memory of them forgotten. (Eccl. 9:5)

I chose to walk in the light instead of the darkness.

I rebuilt my moral compass by using the heavenly Father's instruction manual. I broke the chain of bondage and self-sabotage with his Word and overcame the smears of death.

ABOUT THE AUTHOR

Maki Jahana, a direct descendant of the Maroon tribe, migrated to Canada to join her mother at eleven when her community was impacted by crime and violence. By age sixteen, she was so resilient she applied to the Canadian Citizen Board and became a Canadian. She is a mother of four and a grateful grandmother of three.

Printed in the United States
by Baker & Taylor Publisher Services